PRAISE FOR *10 MILLION TO 1*

"I absolutely love this book. Jeffrey Kirk provides great balance between real, practical advice, and inspirational, emotional stories; completely covering the intricacies of resettlement, empowering these people as people, and not treating them as victims. Refugee Resettlement agencies nationwide should use this book as their guide to create, improve, and evaluate their model of volunteer engagement. It's an absolute must read for anyone interested in working or volunteering with refugees during their resettlement process."

Benjamin York
Community Resource Coordinator
Lutheran Social Services of Wisconsin and Upper Michigan

"Refugee resettlement is something that can become a considerable passion for many of us who discover it. *10 Million To 1* is organized in a way that will allow it to serve many groups interested in developing such programs. It will be very helpful in modeling best practices for those interested in co-sponsorship programs as well as refugee resettlement in general."

Daniel S. Amick, PhD
Associate Professor & Chair, Department of Anthropology
Loyola University, Chicago, IL

"*10 Million To 1* is a comprehensive guide to one of the most powerful and touching volunteer opportunities in the United States, refugee resettlement. Mr. Kirk's passion and knowledge about the subject is clear and provides co-sponsors with a great opportunity to avoid commonly encountered mistakes."

Claire Herzog
Refugee Sponsorship Developer, Omaha, NE

"*10 Million To 1* is a must-read for anyone with an interest in refugee resettlement. Jeff focuses on the most important part of resettlement—the goal of self-sufficiency for each refugee that makes a new life in the United States. While each refugee's story is unique, Jeff's stories and explanations in the book take away the uncertainty of resettlement and should encourage citizens to reach out and become involved."

Jen Huber
Apex, NC (previously worked with refugees in Phoenix, AZ)

"WOW! I think Jeffrey Kirk has done a wonderful job covering all the bases. I definitely could have used this book a year ago! I think this book will help anyone who wants to get started in helping these precious people!"

Wendy Fields
Director of The Karenni Konnection
English Professor at Robeson Community College,
Lumberton, NC

"What an excellent resource! I wish I would have had access to it last April. Having it to refer to would have made things so much easier! I'm sure it will be a big help to refugee resettlement committees everywhere."

Donna Tredrea
Refugee Resettlement Committee,
Pilgrim United Church of Christ, Grafton, WI

"*10 Million To 1* is a roadmap for refugee resettlement that reads as easy as a captivating novel. Amen to Jeffrey Kirk's advice on resettlement: 'Just do it!' That counsel, along with this inspiring guidebook, came out of his firsthand experience creating from scratch a very successful resettlement ministry at Ascension Lutheran Church. This adventure in hospitality changes more than the lives of refugees who are given a new, secure life. At Ascension, it has been changing our congregation: passion for ministry has grown; compassion for and understanding of people from other cultures has deepened; and joy in being partners with God in building a global community of peace has increased greatly. So, just do it! This wonderful book will show you how."

Frank Janzow
Lead Pastor, Ascension Lutheran Church, Waukesha, WI

"*10 Million To 1* answers so many questions that those involved in refugees' lives have. As personnel in local businesses, community organizations, churches, schools, and health facilities become increasingly aware of the needs of the refugee population, natural concerns arise. Mr. Kirk, while approaching each concern with respect and cultural sensitivity, comprehensively answers these questions from a variety of legal, economic, humanitarian, religious, and logical perspectives. I would recommend this book to everyone who has ever met a refugee, and I plan to suggest that the entire faculty at my school read it!"

Angela Wade
ESOL/Newcomer Teacher to Refugees, San Antonio, TX

10 MILLION TO 1

10 MILLION TO 1
REFUGEE RESETTLEMENT – A HOW-TO GUIDE

JEFFREY KIRK

BALBOA.
PRESS

A DIVISION OF HAY HOUSE

Balboa Press books may be ordered through booksellers or by contacting:

Balboa Press
A Division of Hay House
1663 Liberty Drive
Bloomington, IN 47403
www.balboapress.com
1-(877) 407-4847

Because of the dynamic nature of the Internet, any web addresses or links contained in this book may have changed since publication and may no longer be valid. The views expressed in this work are solely those of the author and do not necessarily reflect the views of the publisher, and the publisher hereby disclaims any responsibility for them.

The author of this book does not dispense medical advice or prescribe the use of any technique as a form of treatment for physical, emotional, or medical problems without the advice of a physician, either directly or indirectly. The intent of the author is only to offer information of a general nature to help you in your quest for emotional and spiritual well-being. In the event you use any of the information in this book for yourself, which is your constitutional right, the author and the publisher assume no responsibility for your actions.

ISBN: 978-1-4525-3588-3 (e)
ISBN: 978-1-4525-3587-6 (sc)

Library of Congress Control Number: 2011910515

Printed in the United States of America

Balboa Press rev. date: 7/20/2011

CONTENTS

PREFACE

10,000,000 to 1? Long odds? For or against? No, not odds at all, but rather, attitude. There are somewhere in the neighborhood of 10 million refugees in the world today. The problem is staggering, but not impossible to fix. This book is about refugee resettlement, helping one family break free from their label of refugee. Working together, in small groups, we can focus on one family at a time. Your group, my group, and other groups around the world can each focus on helping a single family. Then we do it again with another family. With more groups, more action is taken. Repeat the process until all 10 million refugees can either go home or have a new home.

The first time that refugee resettlement crossed into my realm of consciousness was in 1998 or 1999. One morning at a business networking breakfast, Bill spoke about refugee resettlement instead of talking about his business. He said that he was a volunteer ambassador for LIRS, Lutheran Immigration and Refugee Service. His task was to help find church groups, of any denomination, that would be willing to help sponsor incoming refugee families. His descriptions of refugees and the resettlement process intrigued me. While I love to travel abroad, I was excited that refugee resettlement offered an opportunity to learn more about the world without leaving home. What I didn't realize was how much I would learn.

In 2001, I attended the Milwaukee Synod Assembly for the ELCA, Evangelical Lutheran Church in America. Bill was there with representatives from Lutheran Social Services talking to attendees about the plight of refugees, and what we can do to help. Again, the thoughts pulled at me. I did nothing but consider that, some day, our church should get involved.

Not too long after this, maybe just a couple months, again at my regular business networking breakfast, Bill commented that there were refugee families coming and no churches lined up to help out. He wondered if I could exert any influence at my church. I said I would try and then made a few phone calls. The social concerns committee for our church was going to be meeting soon and they put Bill as a guest speaker on the agenda.

Our social concerns committee was not interested in taking on another activity, but they thought someday this might be a good idea. I don't know if Bill sensed it, or if it was a regular course of action, or if the Holy Spirit was active in that moment. Whatever the reason, Bill pulled out a brief written biography of a family that needed our help. Suddenly we had a family with names and ages. That made it real. While the social concerns committee could not take this on, they said I was free to do so.

It was time to get busy putting a team together to help this family. We planned to help this one Bosnian family start a new life in southeastern Wisconsin. Then we would pat ourselves on the back having done a good job and hope someone else came along for the next family. Reality didn't work out that way. We were hooked. How can you ignore the satisfaction of truly making a difference in the world? Of *being* a difference in the world? We went into refugee resettlement thinking we might be able to help someone. In the end, we were part of a flow of blessings, giving and receiving, participating and feeling, involved and absorbing. What could be better?

From my initial exposure to refugee resettlement, to our co-sponsorship of our first family, 2 to 3 years had elapsed. My hope is that you don't wait that long. If you're reading this book, this how-to-guide, take the advice of those commercials that say "just do it." The need is out there. We have abundant gifts to share in our country; this country built on the backs of our forefathers, most of whom were immigrants and refugees themselves.

After our first family was self-sufficient, we did celebrate a job well done. But we didn't just hope that someone else came along to fill the next need. We went back to work and helped another family. And we're continuing because the need hasn't gone away yet. So I pray that you too will come to see the blessings of refugee resettlement and work to give people a home, and, more importantly, hope. Thirty down, 9,999,970 to go!

As you read the book, please also understand that I am not advocating that we resettle 10 million refugees into the United States, that we empty the world's refugee camps on our shores. Not at all. Rather I believe that there is a solution to the world's refugee problem. It involves foreign refugee resettlement for some, return to their native home for others, education for most, and change or influence in the countries that are "producing" refugees – so that the problem is reduced in the future.

I do not know all the answers, but I do believe the answers are out there. We just have to be open to finding them. In the meantime, this book is designed to help refugees, and their resettlement volunteers, be as successful as possible.

One final note as you head into the chapters that follow, each chapter begins with a first-person story in the life of a real refugee experience. You will find neither their names nor their countries represented. This is to provide anonymity for the refugees in their new life as well as protection for their friends and family back home. Some have been fearful that even little bits of information could bring trouble to those they love. I respect their wishes so that you may read their words.

ACKNOWLEDGMENTS

I am grateful to Lutheran Social Services in Milwaukee for introducing me to the basics of the methodology that I describe in this book. Specifically I must say thank-you to Bill Duke who I brought up in the Preface. Without Bill's presence, bringing the stories and his experience with LIRS, I would not have received the inspiration to move forward. I also thank Susan Gundlach who worked for LSS in Milwaukee at the time and now works for LIRS in Maryland. Susan's expertise helped us get off on the right foot when we were new at this resettlement thing. Her praise along the way also encouraged us to go further and help more.

As this book came together, I had the opportunity to have an earlier draft of the manuscript reviewed by Larry Yungk, Senior Resettlement Officer of UNHCR. Larry's commentary was significant in helping me more fully understand and communicate to you the initial resettlement process and the interaction between UNHCR and the U.S. governmental entities. Additionally, Katherine Evans of the International Rescue Committee took time to write up notes giving me perspective from another of the Volags. Ben York of LSS in Milwaukee was also a good source of inspiration, as we had a number of resettlement conversations that helped me clarify some points within. And, what good is an acknowledgment section without giving some credit to one's mother? My mom, Sue Kirk, offered encouragement along the way and helped tremendously by reviewing and editing an early copy.

I'd like to thank other churches and the people there who have allowed my wife and me to talk about our experiences. One of the greatest ways to learn is to teach. By helping other churches get their resettlement programs going, I've learned so much more than if I had only gone through the resettlement process at our church. By understanding their questions and providing answers, I've been able to enhance the details you'll find in this book.

Now it is imperative that I express my gratitude to the many members of the resettlement teams at Ascension Lutheran Church. Amanda Tenwinkel was one of the first to jump on board with the first family we took on. She handled many of the details along with my wife when we were first trying to understand what we had gotten ourselves into. Buck Houston was integral in getting through the process for several of the early families, even jumping in to take the reins for a time. Iva Richards has been a constant, always available to help. She digs in one family after another, especially sitting through countless appointments of all kinds. And, Jo Buth has provided help for the Burmese families above and beyond any expectation. Jo started working with Burmese refugees before I was even aware of refugee resettlement, and she continues to this day.

There are many others in the past decade who have helped on one committee or another; offering time for driving to appointments, finding and delivering furniture, schooling, training and tutoring both adults and children, helping with job searches, driving to new jobs, grocery shopping, and much more. Some of the faithful contributors who provided significant help for several families include Barb Sand, Bill Tenwinkel, Dick Williams, Jane and Mark Blackman, Kathryn Murphy, Marsha James, and Paula Bickel. I know there are many more who helped at one time or another, some even building great friendships with our refugee families. To identify everyone who played a part would probably fill this page. Please know you are still important even if I did not list your name. Your questions, comments, and actions all helped the successful outcomes of the families you touched.

Of course, the list from church would not be complete without thanking the pastors who have been so supportive and encouraging of our efforts. I truly appreciate Pastor Frank Janzow and Pastor Jim Bickel for allowing us the freedom to do what was necessary to get the job done right. We tried to involve them as little as possible knowing that they had many other things on their plates as pastors at a growing church. I'm sure their prayers and blessings on our activities helped to keep us moving down the right path.

Most of all I have to thank my wife, the number one love of my life, Bryn. Without her, none of this would have gone anywhere. We joke about all the things I get her into. Well this is a big one. For most of the families we've resettled, she and I have been co-chairs. And, when I haven't been a co-chair she still has been, often taking the lead. We've been a great team working together. She has also previewed everything in this book to confirm I'm telling it like it is. Of course, I should also acknowledge our children, Alexander and Victoria, who have put up with this craziness for the better part of their lives. With each family we resettle, they have to give up some time with us. And sometimes they give up part of our house too. Yet I hope the example they see, as we proactively create a better world, is a strong series of lessons from which they can learn.

YOUR STORY

THE BEGINNING...

Imagine for a moment that you are a refugee. You have lived in the same community your entire life. It's roughly the same place your family has lived for generations. Suddenly, a military dictator rises up and everything changes. You find yourself part of an ethnic group that is considered an undesirable minority. You are the target of extermination. First, you think you'll get through it. You'll survive. Bad things happen to other people. Then the police raid your home and take many of your possessions. Your children are assaulted. You are beaten. One of your neighbors was killed. What to do? You flee!

Somehow, you and your family manage to escape with your lives to a neighboring country. The natives take you in, but they don't really want you. There's a camp. At least it's a place to stay. It's not home, but you don't feel an immediate threat on your life. There's no way to earn a living. It's tough to get regular meals. It's hard to stay dry in the rain. It's miserable, and all you want to do is go back home, but you're not welcome there. So you stay in the camp to remain alive and you keep the hope that someday you will go home.

Years go by. Your survival instincts are fine-tuned. Your children hardly remember life outside the camp. You realize they have no future.

You still long for home, but the hope you had has faded. Now you just want a chance at a "normal" life. Isn't there a way to escape the daily anguish without putting your life and those you love at greater risk? Then, it happens. You are given a chance to leave the camp for another country, a country that will take you in, welcome you, and help you start over.

You are scared, but you want to provide for your family. You want them to have a chance. You know the rest of your life may be difficult, but at least it's moving out of the stagnant situation you've been in. At least, for the first time in a long time, there is a glimmer of hope.

At long last you get on an airplane bound for the United States. You've heard good things, and you've heard bad things. You've heard of prosperity, and you've heard of neglect. You're excited, but you are headed into another unknown. What will your new life hold for you? Whom will you meet? How will you communicate when you don't know English? At least you understand life in a refugee camp. But here, now, landing in the U.S. you know nothing...

Now you, as the reader of this book, have the privilege to step out of the role of the refugee. That's not your life. But did you get a brief glimpse of what the refugee was feeling? What would you want if you were in that situation? What would you need? If you were the one landing in the U.S. with your family, wouldn't you enjoy being met by someone offering you help, offering you direction, offering you love? Absolutely.

CHAPTER 1

WHO ARE REFUGEES?

I was enjoying the afternoon with some of my friends. Suddenly a bomb exploded in our midst. I was, quite literally, blown up. We were all taken away as dead.

In the morgue they discovered that I was still alive. With repeated surgeries, and over a year in the hospital, I was put back together and I was able to walk out. But then I was taken away from my family and held as a prisoner in my homeland. Eventually, with the help of my family, I was able to escape. We fled, becoming refugees. We were separated from friends and family, but at least we were together. We were admitted to the U.S. to start our lives again. With five and a half years in our new home, I became a citizen, thankful for the opportunity for myself, my wife, and my children.

Defining refugees

A refugee is a person who "owing to a well-founded fear of being persecuted for reasons of race, religion, nationality, membership of a particular social group, or political opinion, is outside the country of

his nationality and is unable, or owing to such fear, is unwilling to avail himself of the protection of that country."
–   *The 1951 Geneva Refugee Convention*

A refugee is "any person who is outside any country of such person's nationality or, in the case of a person having no nationality, is outside any country in which such person last habitually resided, and who is unable or unwilling to return to, and is unable or unwilling to avail himself or herself of the protection of, that country because of persecution or a well-founded fear of persecution on account of race, religion, nationality, membership in a particular social group, or political opinion."
–   *U.S. Refugee Act of 1980*

The one place most people long for is home. To summarize the above definitions, a refugee is someone who cannot go home or is afraid to go home. For refugees, their home is taken away, suddenly, and often by force. Since they must travel quickly and light, they leave the bulk of their possessions behind. They flee to a neighboring country where they may face inhospitable conditions, overcrowded refugee camps, few services, and little welcome. In a short time, they lose their previous lives, their possessions, their friends, and even their families.

There are far too many refugees in the world today. At the beginning of 2011, the United Nations High Commissioner for Refugees (UNHCR) recognized roughly 10.3 million refugees of concern to their organization. These refugees are found all around the world, with more than half in Asia and about 20 percent in Africa. As refugees, they live in a variety of different conditions, from well-established camps to makeshift shelters to roaming without shelter. More than half live in urban areas.

It is important to note in light of ongoing immigration discussions, that when refugees arrive in the U.S. they are not illegal immigrants. They do not sneak across our borders in the dark of night. They are not undocumented workers. They do not have to lie about their status or hide from authorities. They arrive in our country by following a lengthy, fully-documented legal process by which they receive most rights and benefits of natural citizens.

How do the refugees get to the United States?

Once the refugees are outside of their home country they are interviewed by staff of the U.N. High Commissioner for Refugees. The UNHCR staff will determine the refugees' status. If they meet the criteria, they are officially documented as refugees and are allowed to remain in the new country. In many situations refugees can live among the people within their new country, but often, due to a large influx of refugees, or economic conditions, or population resentment, or a variety of other conditions within the receiving country, it is necessary for refugees to live in camps.

Whether in camps or living among the citizens, the refugees may wait in limbo for months or years. Sometimes they are able to return home (repatriation). Sometimes they are able to make new lives for themselves in the country where they have taken refuge (local integration). Sometimes they may have to continue living in the harsh conditions of a refugee camp that is overcrowded, has insufficient or inadequate food and water supplies, lacks privacy, suffers from poor sanitation and medical care, and offers little opportunity for education or income generation. This confinement becomes especially problematic if the refugees have to live there for many years, unable to maintain a normal lifestyle.

But sometimes resettlement in another country is possible! While this last option is currently available for less than 1% of all refugees, it is the reason this book was written. Resettlement in a third country opens up possibilities for refugees to begin new lives.

Here is an overview of the process that is followed in the United States...

Each year the President of the United States consults with Congress and other appropriate agencies to set a quota on the number of refugees who will be allowed to resettle in the U.S. for that year. Not only is there a limit on the total number, but the President may also set a limit on the number of refugees that will be permitted to enter the U.S. from specific parts of the world. Specific nationalities are designated, and processing priorities are established. Then the U.S. Department of State administers the refugee resettlement program. The State Department, using the established guidelines and priorities, determines which refugee cases are eligible for resettlement.

Once eligibility is established, their case moves to the Department of Homeland Security (DHS), and more specifically to the staff of the US Citizenship and Immigration Service (USCIS). Here they review each case. Applicants for refugee admission into the United States must meet all of the following criteria:

- They must meet the definition of a refugee contained in the Immigration and Nationality Act;
- They must be a member of a refugee group determined by the President to be of special humanitarian concern to the United States;
- They must be otherwise admissible under United States law;
- They must not be already firmly resettled in any foreign country.

Once DHS/USCIS approves a case, it goes back to the State Department. The State Department finishes reviewing all other requirements specific to each individual case. These specific requirements include a health evaluation, security screening, an evaluation of potential sponsorship of the refugee family, suitability for travel, and more.

Now that you have a big picture view of the process, let's dig in a little deeper. The State Department administers this program, but how does a refugee get the attention of the State Department to begin with?

It all starts with a referral. In a general sense, these referrals come about in three ways:

1. An organization can refer a refugee. In this case, usually UNHCR makes the referral. It is also possible that a U.S. Embassy or a qualified Non-Governmental Organization (NGO) can make the referral.

2. A refugee can become eligible because they are part of a group of special concern designated by the U.S.
3. A family member in the U.S. files appropriate sponsorship papers with one of the resettlement agencies or with USCIS.

Each of these three referral methods also corresponds to what the U.S. calls its processing priorities. Priority 1 is almost entirely made up of UNHCR referrals. Out of the potentially thousands of refugees resettled each year in the U.S. only a few hundred may come from Embassy or NGO referrals. Priority 1 processing focuses on individual refugees and refugee families. UNHCR may make referrals for refugees because the refugee is specifically asking to be resettled after registering as a refugee. On the other hand, UNHCR may discover a need during the refugee registration that would best be served by resettlement.

Unlike Priority 1, Priority 2 focuses on persons who are members of specific groups. The UNHCR and U.S. may work together to jointly determine these groups based on specific needs. The U.S. may also designate some groups independently. In either case, the U.S., the President and Congress make this determination. In Priority 2, it is possible that the U.S. will designate someone as a refugee even though they are still in their home country. An example of direct placement may be a Cuban resettled directly from Cuba. If UNHCR refers a group, those are always coming from the second country, the country to which the refugee fled. An example of this would be Burmese refugees within the camps of Thailand. However, just because they are part of the group does not mean they will be resettled automatically. Resettlement is never forced. In other words, an ethnic Burmese living in a Thai camp must still express an interest in resettlement before anything else can happen.

Priority 3 is rather limited. This method rarely involves UNHCR because the refugee gets into the process simply because they have a close relative in the U.S. who has filed the sponsorship forms. Since there are other immigration options for family members of those who live in the U.S., this method is limited to only a few nationalities.

When the referral comes in, the State Department uses an Overseas Processing Entity (OPE). This is often an NGO. The organization that we've seen used in every case has been the International Organization for Migration (IOM), though others are possible. The staff of the OPE prepares the cases for the DHS interview. They double-check that the case is eligible and that it fits one of the three processing priorities.

Assuming all is well up to this point, the refugees are approved, and the case moves over to DHS/USCIS for further scrutiny. During the interview process, the refugees still have to prove their refugee status is legitimate. They will have to meet all the other requirements already discussed as well. Failure to meet the criteria at any point results in the rejection of their refugee settlement case.

Finally, after waiting, and interviewing, and waiting some more, those approved for admission into the U.S. are assigned to one of the 11 resettlement agencies that have agreements with the U.S. Department of State. The agencies that participate in the Refugee Admissions Reception and Placement Program under a cooperative agreement with the U.S. State Department are:

- Church World Service (www.churchworldservice.org)
- Episcopal Migration Ministries (www.ecusa.anglican.org/emm)
- Ethiopian Community Development Council (www.ecdcinternational.org)
- Hebrew Immigrant Aid Society (www.hias.org)
- International Rescue Committee (www.theirc.org)
- Kurdish Human Rights Watch (www.khrw.org)
- Lutheran Immigration and Refugee Services (www.lirs.org)
- State of Iowa, Bureau of Refugee Services (www.dhs.state.ia.us/refugee)
- United States Conference of Catholic Bishops (www.nccbuscc.org/mrs)
- US Committee for Refugees and Immigrants (www.refugees.org)
- World Relief Corporation (www.wr.org)

These 11 agencies, often called Volags (for Voluntary Agencies), receive some of their funding through the State Department's Bureau of Population, Refugees, and Migration (PRM). Typically, this funding lasts for the first 90 days of the resettlement process. The Volags may also contract with the Office of Refugee Resettlement (ORR), which *Connect Families* is part of the U.S. Department of Health and Human Services, for a variety of social services funding. This funding can extend for up to five years.

The assigned agency will decide where the refugees will go within the U.S. The organization must abide by State Department supervision and rules, but within those guidelines, the agency has freedom to choose. They will look at things like where others in their ethnic group are located, whether they have relatives already in the U.S., where housing and employment are available, where appropriate services can be obtained, and even where volunteer support is ready to help.

Individuals and families that are ultimately granted refugee status by the U.S. are provided medical examinations, inoculations, and any necessary treatments to prepare for their departure. The Department of State strives to ensure that refugees accepted for admission to the United States are prepared for the significant changes they will experience during the resettlement process. It is important that, prior to departure, refugees have a realistic understanding of what their new lives will be like, what services are available to help them, and what their responsibilities will be. All refugees should have this basic information before stepping onto U.S. soil.

In the end, only a small number of refugees (less than ½ of 1%) make it to the United States. Since the enactment of the Refugee Act of 1980, annual admissions to the U.S. have ranged from a low of 27,128 in Fiscal Year 2002 to a high of 207,116 in 1980. The average number admitted annually since 1980 is about 83,400. While these numbers are significant, our efforts are small compared to the very large problem. Yet, even a single successful resettlement is an accomplishment worth celebrating!

At the U.S. port of entry, USCIS admits each refugee to the United States and immediately authorizes employment, a necessary step to help ensure self-sufficiency. After one year, a refugee is eligible, and required, to apply for a change of status to lawful permanent resident. That is, they can obtain a Green Card. Four years and nine months after admission, a refugee is eligible to apply for citizenship via naturalization.

CHAPTER 2

RESETTLING REFUGEES

A bomb exploded in our kitchen. My husband and son were killed. I was injured. Suddenly I was a single mom with four daughters. It's not safe for women without husbands here, especially a pregnant woman with young girls. So we fled to a neighboring country. My new son was born in the refugee camp where we then lived for four years before coming to the United States.

Why Resettle Refugees?

"For you created my inmost being; you knit me together in my mother's womb. I praise you because I am awesomely and wonderfully made." Psalm 139:13-14a

Look at the faces of refugees, study them, and see the uniqueness that is theirs. Look into their hearts to see what life was for them before, and what it is now. Look into their souls and you can still see the beauty that God put there. Look into their eyes now, and odds are you see a look of hope. While unfortunate circumstances made them refugees, that does not change the fact that God made them as wonderful individuals.

Refugees are people who have been denied the chance to live a "normal" life. Things in their lives have gotten so bad that they have felt forced to leave their own country. A person does not wake up one day and decide to become a refugee. Rather, they feel their life depends on fleeing their home, possibly their family, and everything they've ever known.

Most refugees are good people, willing to do anything they can to establish normalcy in their lives. If they can get away from the persecution, and threat of persecution, they can develop into contributing members of society. Yet, while they maintain refugee status in the overburdened countries they have fled to, there is little opportunity. When another country steps in to resettle a refugee or refugee family, a problem is reduced. Anxiety is diminished. A step toward peace is taken. Poverty, hunger, and disease are lessened. With every refugee that can find a new home, the world is a slightly better place.

So, this all sounds really good in theory, but ultimately the decision to resettle refugees doesn't end with governments. It ends with people. It comes down to your decision to help. Refugees come from all over the world. We can't just bring them to the front door of our own country and expect them to fit right in. They need help. They need to understand our country, our society, our customs, and our cultural idiosyncrasies. They need to know all the things we learned as we grew from children into adults. They need to understand how to live in a manner that allows them to belong.

If you are going to help refugees make it in your community, you need personal reasons to offer help. Your personal reasons may be that you want to be an advocate for world peace or fight to alleviate hunger and poverty, or your reasons may be much more personal. Perhaps you simply want to learn about a different culture without leaving the comfort of home. Instead of traveling the world, you'd rather bring the world to you. Maybe you want a good excuse to learn a new language. Maybe you like to teach. Maybe you think that doing something good will make a difference and feel good too. Maybe logic drives your actions, and you have concluded that helping refugees is just the right thing to do. Maybe you just have an intense love for other people. Maybe you've experienced a spiritual calling.

It doesn't really matter, with a few exceptions, what your personal motivations are, but it is important that you have reasons. While refugee resettlement is rewarding, it is not always easy. Having concrete reasons why you want to do this, along with a long-term vision of a positive outcome, can help you get through the tougher times. Developing those reasons into a passion to serve will carry you through the entire process and give you confidence that you can make a difference in our world today.

Wrong Reasons to Resettle

There are some reasons that should not be the basis of your resettlement activities. Obviously there should be no criminal intent, or desire to take advantage of people in need. There should also be no expectation of personal gain. You should not get involved with refugee resettlement if your expectation is a tangible reward for yourself. You should also think twice about resettlement if you will have a tendency to want others to be dependent upon you, if you tend to create codependency relationships, or if you have a desire to join or control another family. Remember the goal is to help create a self-sufficient family. That won't happen if you create any dependency in either direction.

In many cases, church groups handle refugee resettlement. You should not view the resettlement of a refugee family as a means to increase church membership or to force your beliefs on other people. Church and religious groups that wish to work with refugees are best advised to respect the beliefs of the refugees they work with. My own refugee experience has been through our church. While we are Christian, we have resettled four families of Islamic tradition (though not necessarily active in their faith). We are able to demonstrate our beliefs through our loving actions. After the families had a chance to settle in, we invited them to our church for a special day in their honor so that all of those at church who supported the efforts could meet them. We even offered the refugee families the opportunity to prepare food of their culture to share. The event was all about our refugee families, not about our church.

Outside Resistance

As you work with refugees, you'll become aware of several arguments against refugee resettlement. The longer you are involved in refugee work, the more likely you are to hear these things, and the nastier some of them will be.

"There are people in our own community that need help." "Shouldn't we focus on helping the homeless in our own town?" "What about helping out with veterans who proudly served our country?" "Speaking of our country, we worked hard to create it and protect it, and now we just give the benefits away to other people who don't deserve it." "America should be for Americans." "We have to pay taxes to support these people." "Immigrants take away jobs that our own people could be working." "If we open the doors, we'll have 4 billion people living in the United States and we can't support that." The list goes on.

While I cannot possibly address every negative comment you might hear, I can attempt to frame things to help you deflect these comments and prevent them from derailing your efforts.

What about helping people who are already living in our own community, state, region, and country? Absolutely. People have to be concerned about these things. However, those don't have to be the same people that work on refugee resettlement. It is important to take care of neighbors wherever they are located. So what is your calling? How far does your definition of "neighbor" extend? Do you feel you should be helping refugees, or should you work with the homeless in your own town? Find your passion. If your passion is to work with the less fortunate somewhere else, then refugee resettlement may be for you. Offer encouragement to those who push you to help locally. Help them make it their passion to take on these important activities. If they are active in the community, then all interests are served. If they just want you to change your focus, but they aren't helping anyway, then who are they to talk? You're making a positive change in the world and they're trying to live on the benefits.

What about giving our benefits to those who didn't earn them or keeping America for Americans? To these comments, I wonder where these people came from such that their ancestors arrived in America without immigrating. The people making this argument forget that they are descendants of immigrants. What if the somewhat younger America had refused to accept their family? America has never been a homogeneous people. In our entire history, we have allowed others to enter. This diversity has helped bless our country with growth and prosperity through the years.

What about our taxes supporting refugees or the potential for them to take away jobs from Americans? Keep in mind that the goal of refugee resettlement, at least as defined in this book, is not to add people to the welfare rolls of your state. The goal is to help the family become self-sufficient in the shortest time possible. Within several months, the family members should have jobs and be contributing to our society, paying taxes like the rest of us. As for jobs, it is often the immigrants, including refugees, who take the necessary low-wage positions that others don't want. When the economy is in good shape, low-wage jobs are abundant. Filling these positions with people willing to accept the conditions is of great benefit to the employers as well as the recent refugee families. It's a win-win situation. When the economy is in poor condition, and others are being laid off, many low-wage positions are still available because those who were laid off would rather go on welfare than stoop to take a low-wage position. It's a matter of attitude. Refugees are generally willing to work with any employer that will take them. The average Americans, who are descendants of refugees and other immigrants, have higher expectations and, often, greater feelings of entitlement.

Finally, what about the argument that 4 billion people will want to come to America? Anyone who says this clearly loves his or her country and expects that everyone else does too. Let's put this into perspective. I might think that a smooth dark chocolate candy bar is the best food in the world. If I had a small supply, I might want to hoard it, afraid that surely everyone else is going to try to get it. The reality is that while others may agree with my assessment, plenty of people do not. The same is true with living in America. We enjoy it, love it, defend it, promote it, but that doesn't mean that everyone else necessarily wants to live here. Everyone just wants to live in a place they can call home. Keep in mind that a refugee's first choice is to move back to their home, wherever it was. That's the place they long for, their place of familiarity and comfort. They choose the option of moving to the United States only after all other options failed. With some caring and some luck, they will eventually regard our country as their home. At that time, they will be as American as the rest of us.

Also, keep in mind that those who tend to resist your efforts, or bring up arguments against refugee resettlement, may have valid reasons for doing so. Not all resettlement efforts around the country have gone the way they should. When something goes wrong, and it makes the news, many people are exposed to a single negative situation without realizing many of the good outcomes that often occur but go unnoticed. In other cases, people simply misunderstand the distinction between illegal immigrants sneaking into the country and refugees who come via legitimate channels. And in other cases you'll encounter those who have a poor impression of government programs. They may make some good points too. No matter what the resistance, the dialog is important. By talking through the issues, we can all learn and improve the situation.

The key point for you, as you begin a refugee resettlement project, is to not be distracted by the resistance, but it is important for you to think through the issues. The questions will come up, and you'll have an easier time explaining your position if you've thought these things through in advance. The best time to have an in depth conversation, however, is after you've had some success. Then you are able to speak from direct experience and potentially help define the changes that would make the process better.

CHAPTER 3

GETTING STARTED

We converted to Christianity in an Islamic country. Our families no longer wanted to be associated with us because it meant certain hardship for them. Eventually, I was thrown in jail. My wife was told that I was killed. Can you imagine the stress that caused her?

After some time she learned that I was still alive. She rallied others to an uproar and secured my release, though the pressure and stress continued. Abandoned by friends and family, and mounting political and religious pressures, we had to flee for our lives. In the neighboring country we met missionaries who helped us seek refugee status. We were nearly deported back to our home country, again because of our religion, but we managed to get out in time, coming to the United States. We miss our family, but they are safer without us. Now that we're gone, we can comfortably talk to them on the phone.

Imagine that you have decided to help refugees start a new life in your community. Where do you begin? What do you have to learn? What services are available? How will you figure out "the system?" How will you get people to help you?

Now imagine you are a refugee. You have just arrived in a new country. Everything is different now. The language, the culture, the laws are all unfamiliar. How can you expect to get a job? How will you get your children into schools? How are you even going to find a place to live?

You see, your situation is easier than the refugees' situation. You know your community. You have friends that will help you. You may not know "the system" but you can communicate in your own language, asking questions to find out the answers. You are the lifeline making the refugees' impossible situation into a workable reality. Your existing knowledge is enough to help them with their adjustments. Your lifetime of experience is enough to help them survive and even thrive in a new world. In addition, you have this book. By the time you complete reading it, you will have a good understanding of what it takes to handle the resettlement process.

Refugee resettlement does require some commitment. While the 11 agencies presented in Chapter 1 are the sponsors of the refugees, many depend on co-sponsors and other volunteers to assist in the resettlement process. Each refugee family has specific needs upon their arrival. Often, people who live and work in the community can better handle those needs than the agency can alone. Local churches and other dedicated groups can provide much more contact with a refugee family. That contact helps the family achieve self-sufficiency faster and helps to demonstrate human love and kindness, coming from strangers, which may have been missing from their lives for years. Furthermore, the personal relationships that develop between the co-sponsors and the refugee family provide a connection to help them feel at home. You become their advocates and their friends.

Before you meet the refugees, your primary questions will revolve around the issue of "what are we getting into?" While the real answer to that question will play out over time, there are some things you will need to consider. As a co-sponsor, your group is agreeing to help a family become self-sufficient, contributing members of your community in the shortest possible time. That effort takes time and money, the two main things you'll be worried about at first.

First, let's look at the money question. How much is this going to cost? Your group should be prepared to assume financial responsibility for a minimum of 1 to 2 months. From that point on the financial needs will diminish. The speed of decline is determined by both the level of public assistance in your community and the job prospects for the employable members of the family.

Then, there's the time commitment. How much time will this take? The bulk of the time requirement happens quickly upon the family's arrival. You will see in the details to follow that there are many activities taking place to get the family started on the right foot. Many of the initial activities are completed within the first couple of weeks of arrival. This will be the busiest period for your resettlement team. You could plan on about 250 person-hours of time from the moment the family arrives at the airport, to the completion of the first month.

Everything is new to your refugee family at this time so they need lots of support. They will have various medical and dental appointments and school registrations. They will have to start learning about using community services and paying for public utilities. They will have to deal with culture shock and adjusting to life in our country. Nothing they do is habitual. They have to think about everything.

To put this in perspective think about your travels to a foreign country. Whether you've done that once or dozens of times, there is always something nice about coming home. When you come home, you can operate out of instinct. You don't have to think about every action you take during the course of a day. It just comes natural. While you were in the foreign land, you had to concentrate so much harder. It may have been exciting, but it was much more exhausting. Your refugee family will feel this pressure every day, only they won't be going home. This is their home now. During their first month, your time and your effort help to make it their home. You are helping them create new habits so that this land becomes comfortable to them.

The second month will cut that effort level to one half or one third the initial level. In the third month, your effort may drop in half again. Your mentoring relationship will continue for about six months, maybe a little less, maybe up to year. After that point you or some in your group, may have become good friends of the family and will have developed a lasting relationship.

It is good to have realistic expectations of what is going to happen throughout the resettlement process. That is the basis of this book. While it is important to learn about the process so that you can be well prepared, refugee resettlement is much like having children. If you wait until you know everything first, you'll never move forward. The depth of this book is far beyond the information we knew when we sponsored our first family. Upon completion of your reading, consider yourself a graduate of Resettlement College. You will have all the concepts, so get to work!

Besides the two primary issues of time and money, here are some other things to expect. First, and foremost, things will not always happen as planned. We're all human. Most likely, you're running this as a committee, and we all know how committees operate. Furthermore, different languages are involved as well as different cultures. There is plenty of room for miscommunication and misunderstanding. Get over it, and just resolve to be flexible.

You might discover that you are anxious about helping. You've never done anything like this before. What if you don't know what to say? What if you can't communicate what you want to say? What if you are together in a car sitting in silence? Most of us working with refugees come to these points from time to time. It's OK. Odds are that the refugee family feels the same. They might not know what to say or know how to say it. They might have never met an American before. Just push forward and you'll develop a good working relationship that may evolve into friendship.

One thing that can be difficult in building that relationship is a preconceived notion of what the other person is going to be like. The family you are receiving is probably not a group of stereotypical <*insert country or ethnic name here*> persons. They are unique. You will have to discover them. Likewise, they probably have some preconceived notions of the United States. They are probably wrong, based on rumors from their childhood or what they've heard said in refugee camps. Imagine if they believe that in America, life is always easy with everything we want handed to us on a silver platter. How shocked will they be to discover that they are going to have to work hard to get ahead?

As the refugee family tries to understand our culture, with your help, they will come to you with questions – many, many questions. You may have to answer the same question several times. They are trying to process the answers with what they already know to make a complete picture. Yet language barriers and the stress of immersion can be confusing. As their big picture develops, the answers will start to make sense reducing the need for such questions as time goes by.

Some of the questions you hear will be requests for things that they want, for example, "can I have a DVD player," "we need a better telephone," "when will you get us a car?" In the beginning, you must assess whether they are making a request based on need or want. In part, you are responsible for their well-being, their adaptation into our society and culture. However, do not feel that you have to give in to every request. You may not be comfortable with the idea at first, but learning to say "no" will pay big dividends later on. As long as you have already provided all the requirements (discussed later in this book) to address the needs, then you have the freedom to say "no" to wants. It's important for you to set boundaries that you and the refugees can understand.

Sometimes the questions will not be based on wants, but will be a request for other types of help. In this case, you will have to decide where to draw the line. Moreover, you will have to feel OK when you are unable to help. Remember that you are guiding the family to self-sufficiency. That means they have to eventually learn to do it all themselves. If they become dependent upon you, then you are not helping them (or yourself) reach that goal. Often more learning and more independence comes from trying to solve their own problems after getting a "no" from you.

At some point, probably very early on, you are likely to become curious of the refugee family's story. After all, we all love a good story! Many refugees come with heartache and pain, tragedy and loss, stories of courage and overcoming unbelievable odds. They might share some of this with you. They might not. Consider it a blessing if you do come to know their story. Do not expect them to tell you. Do not encourage them to do so. When they are ready, if they feel comfortable, then they may open up to you. But, the hardships may have been too great for them to ever want to share their personal story. Respect their decision either way.

Regardless of whether you hear their story or not, you can expect to be changed. The refugee family is experiencing life-changing things, really big life-changing things. You cannot be a part of that without changing too. You will learn new things, feel new things, and discover a place in the world. If your mind is open, be ready for a journey of discovery.

Family Biography – These are Real People

Once you've agreed to co-sponsor a refugee family, you'll await the family's biography. (Sometimes the sponsoring agency may already have a family coming soon, but no co-sponsor assigned. In this case, you will receive a biography as soon as you agree to co-sponsor. Or, in the case of our first family, the biography was used as a tool to get us moving.)

The biography, though containing very limited information, makes the family real. Just knowing the names of the family members, with perhaps their ages and levels of education, will start to draw you into the mode of wanting to help. You don't have a face yet, but the picture starts to develop.

In the case of our first family, we decided it would be a good idea for our church to sponsor a refugee *someday*. Bill, the Lutheran Immigration and Refugee Service ambassador, who was talking to our group, passed out the family biography. If we had said no to this, we wouldn't have simply turned down the concept of sponsoring, but rather we would have rejected this specific family. That did not feel right. Fortunately, with knowledge of a specific refugee family it was also much easier to get additional help. The details, sketchy as they were, made the situation real.

Assemble the Core Support Group

Now that you've decided to sponsor a family, or were pulled in by a family biography, it's time to get to work. One of the first considerations is the size of your resettlement group. How many people does it take to comfortably handle a resettlement? Based on our past experience, best successes, and observations of other resettlement committees, we recommend a group of at least 10 for your resettlement team. With 10 or more, the various tasks can be split up so that the effort is a burden on no one. It is important that one person, or perhaps two, take charge to keep the group organized, on task, and communicating well.

Sometimes we are asked if it is possible for an individual, a couple, or a smaller group to resettle a family. It is possible, but the risk of burnout is much higher. It is quite easy for resettlement activities to consume 150 to 250 person-hours of time during the first month. That's a full-time job for one person. Unless you dedicate your life to resettlement, this is too much. Take that same 200 hours, split it 10 ways, and each person is averaging 5 hours per week. On top of work and family life, this is much more realistic. Several people will put in more than 5 hours per week. Many will put in fewer.

The time investment for the second month should drop to half that of the first month. Activities in the third month should take about a third the time of the first month. How quick the time commitment drops off after that depends on several factors, the greatest of which are employment status, medical conditions, and education concerns.

What types of people should you have as part of your resettlement team? We suggest that you have people in a variety of stages of life. Retired persons can sometimes be more flexible with their time than those of us who work every day. Students are often able to contribute a lot of time during the summers. Mothers and fathers of young children may be more strapped for time, but offer a day-to-day perspective that applies well to refugee families with children. You need organizers, leaders, followers, motivated doers, communicators, and drivers. (Depending on your community and the availability of public transportation or lack of it, you may need many drivers to lessen the load.) Just get a good mix of people and things will work out. One note, don't grab your church pastor or other over-committed church staff. They have enough to do already and will appreciate your team handling the issues without their involvement. Nevertheless, keep them informed and you'll have some good advocates.

Let's go back to that primary big question that every group wants to know. How much does the resettlement effort actually cost? Unfortunately, I cannot give a specific numerical dollar answer. Besides the reasons I've already given, the total will vary depending on the size of the family, the cost of living in your area, and the availability of donated items. You will find other options and considerations below.

As a co-sponsor, one of your responsibilities may be to find and furnish an apartment for the newly arrived refugee family. For every family that we've helped, we called upon the members of our church to donate the needed items. Often, other people in the community would also contribute. People have old furniture they can part with. Others may be moving and will be relieved to not pack and transport their old furnishings. Some may decide to buy new items to contribute. As long as you meet the furnishings requirements, it doesn't matter where the goods come from.

Another responsibility is to provide food for the first 30 days. Getting this food can be something you decide to buy, if your group is well funded, or you can ask for donations as well. Many supermarkets offer prepaid cards that are redeemable for store merchandise. For those who would like to give food, but either don't want to spend time shopping or don't know what to buy, having them buy and donate gifts cards to the local supermarket can be quite helpful.

In most cases, we have had to purchase a few extra items for the apartment. For example, it might not be until move-in day that we learn that some bedroom windows don't have any shades. It's too late to ask for donations because the need is immediate. Therefore, we go buy what we need. Do not put pressure on the members of your resettlement group to pay for these things out of their own pockets. Perhaps they are ready and willing to do so, and, in that case, wonderful! Our attitude has been that those who are part of the core resettlement team are already donating lots of time. Let others donate the money. If the only way to get urgently needed items is to put this on a personal credit card, then so be it. Just be sure to reimburse that person from the donated funds.

You may have some expenses related to furnishings and food during the first month. The big expense, though, is housing, typically apartment rental. In most cases, we pay the first month and security deposit in full. (We are OK with paying one security deposit. If the family chooses to move, they will come up with the next security deposit, but they can keep whatever portion of the original deposit that is returned. Teaching about the security deposit is a good lesson too.) If the refugee family is provided with sufficient funds through the sponsoring organization then we will apply some of this to the earliest months and/or security deposit. This money belongs to the family so we always make sure they retain at least half for other upcoming expenses. While technically this money is theirs to spend as they see fit, you are in a better position to understand their short-term financial needs than they are. Be certain they keep some cash to pay utility bills and other necessary expenses.

After the first couple of months, we assess the rent situation along with the employment status. It is likely that the family will have never paid so much for rent. In fact, they may find the numbers to be staggeringly high. Consider that one month's rent in much of the U.S. can be more than a year's wages for many people. It is difficult to go from paying no rent to paying 100% of a high rent bill, so we have always gradually dropped our contribution while letting the family pay more. The rate of the drop depends on employment and income. Perhaps it will work for you to pay 100% one month, two-thirds the next, one-third the next, and then be done. In other cases, you may pay 100% one month, $100 less the next month, reducing by $100 until complete. Or, you may only be able to work it down to 50% because employment is difficult and whatever assistance the family may receive isn't enough to cover their own food, utilities, other expenses, and full rent.

Be prepared to be flexible with regard to rental expense. In fact, be prepared to be flexible in every step of the process.

Matthew 6:31-33—"*So do not worry, saying, 'What shall we eat?' or 'What shall we drink?' or 'What shall we wear?' For the pagans run after all these things, and your heavenly Father knows that you need them. But seek first his kingdom and his righteousness, and all these things will be given to you as well."*

Declining Support Model

At the beginning, before you dive in with a newly arrived refugee family, be sure your expectations are set correctly. It might help to answer the following questions for yourself. Why do I want to volunteer to help refugees? What will their lives be like when I am done? How much time should I commit to being part of the refugee resettlement committee? Can I say "no" to the family when I need to protect my own time or when they appear to be too dependent? When will my role as volunteer be done? Am I interested in converting to a friendship relationship?

When a refugee family arrives, they will need your help. Their need will diminish over time and it is important that you allow them to become fully self-sufficient. The best analogy to describe what is about to happen is the development of a toddler to adolescence and then to adulthood. It is your job as a co-sponsor to assist in that development. Unlike the growth of your own child, which happens in real-time over many years, your refugee family will make this transition in a period of six months to a year. In the end, you have to let go.

The primary goal of resettlement is to help a refugee family become self-sufficient in as short a time-period as possible. You can coach, encourage, teach, assist, and even carry them when necessary. Yet ultimately, they are independent people who need to live their own lives. In the process, you may become good friends. But, like any good healthy relationship, your friendship should be based on a desire to be friends, not a dependency of one upon the other.

An easy way to think about this is that your support should decrease over time while the refugees' ability to get by in our society increases over time. The adults in your refugee family have been through a lot. They are survivors and have already overcome hardships that we can only imagine. They have lived on their own in the past. They will figure out how to live in our society too. With your help and friendship, they will just learn faster. You will help them navigate the bureaucracies to obtain access to social services, smooth the way for business and financial transactions, and guide them through the process of finding jobs. Most of these things occur in the first couple of months after arrival. Once employment is obtained, usually the last hurdle, support should drop off rapidly.

Within four to six months, if your entire committee has performed its job well, and your refugee family has at least one job, then they should be able to get around, shop, work, go to school, and enjoy life all on their own. They'll be functional, contributing members of society!

Now the fun is about to begin! The next chapter goes into detail on what must be accomplished.

CHAPTER 4

TASKS AND RESPONSIBILITIES

We were in a crowded refugee camp, a human warehouse, for more than 9 years. As bad as it was we were still scared to leave because we heard stories about refugees going to new countries and having bad sponsors. So much uncertainty. We're lucky to have gotten good sponsors.

Every refugee deserves a "good sponsor." That is one of the purposes of this book, helping you understand what it takes to be a good sponsor, to get your refugee family started on the right foot and give hope to other refugees. Keep in mind that their perception of a good sponsor might by accompanied with unrealistic expectations that have been built up in their minds. We're volunteers, doing our best, but we have constraints on our lives too. And, last time I checked, we're still human which means we're not perfect.

In the sections that follow, you will get an understanding of the various roles played in the refugee resettlement process. Each role has certain responsibilities that must be fulfilled for the resettlement to be successful. The sections below are intended to be complete. If you have people for each function, you can successfully manage the resettlement. Depending on the resettlement agency you work with, they may handle some of these tasks themselves. Be sure to check with your sponsoring agency to see which functions they address, and to what level. It doesn't help anyone if you duplicate efforts so try to coordinate your activities. If the agency fulfills a role completely, then you have less to consider.

Resettlement committees can exist in a variety of configurations. It doesn't matter whether you have one person fill one role, or have small teams in each role, or have interested people participate on small teams across several areas. Whatever works for you is OK. It will be most comfortable if you have a core group of eight to twelve people and several others who can help from time to time. What is most important to assess is the amount of time each person can dedicate and how much need the family will have. Clearly, the answer to the family's need is hard to determine until you start working with the family. As a rough guess, for your initial planning purposes, assume the level of effort in the first month will be 125 hours plus 25 hours per person in the family.

The Most Important Thing

When starting to work with a refugee family you may get the feeling that you have to be a problem solver, that your inability to communicate is overwhelming, or that you might just be too uncomfortable to participate. Well, yes, there might be some things outside your comfort zone, but one of those things is really the easiest thing to do. Just be there.

Consider Mark 6:45-51. This story happens right after the familiar story of Jesus feeding 5,000.

"45Immediately Jesus made his disciples get into the boat and go on ahead of him to Bethsaida, while he dismissed the crowd. 46After leaving them, he went up on a mountainside to pray."

"47When evening came, the boat was in the middle of the lake, and he was alone on land. 48He saw the disciples straining at the oars, because the

wind was against them. About the fourth watch of the night he went out to them, walking on the lake. He was about to pass by them, ⁴⁹but when they saw him walking on the lake, they thought he was a ghost. They cried out, ⁵⁰because they all saw him and were terrified."

"Immediately he spoke to them and said, "Take courage! It is I. Don't be afraid." ⁵¹Then he climbed into the boat with them, and the wind died down. They were completely amazed."

The disciples were straining, struggling, in an area of great familiarity. Fishermen know the lake, it's as much their home as the place they lay their heads. Yet they faced fearsome struggles on the lake. After straining most of the night, by the early morning hours they were terrified. In other words, they were terrified, as a group, in their home.

Refugees are much like the disciples in this story. They are coming from a difficult situation. They are struggling against the wind, against forces in the world over which they have no control. Moreover, that struggle began in their homeland.

Next, we have to look at Jesus' role in the story. He started out by praying and then, when the time was right, he went to his disciples. He did not fix their problems by commanding the wind to stop. No, he just got into the boat with them. The problems started going away simply by his presence. When he did speak, it was just to calm their fears. He didn't have to say much. Furthermore, the disciples did not ask Jesus to get in the boat with them. He just did it. He got in the boat because that's what they needed. He was there for them, not for his own needs.

What does this mean for us? We need to be like Jesus when working with refugees. We start out by praying for them. We don't give up even though they may be struggling and fearful. Ultimately, we just have to get in the boat with them and be there for them. Our presence, and only our presence, can be enough to calm the winds.

While the rest of this section delves into specific roles of your refugee committee, remember that the most important thing is simply to be there, in their boat. If you can do that, you're already half done.

Committee and Team Responsibilities

Chairperson or Co-Chairpersons

Every organization needs a leader. Your refugee resettlement group does too. Whether you have a single chairperson, or would prefer to share the responsibilities between chairpersons is up to you. If there is more than one chairperson, it is important that those people work together very closely, such that they are viewed as one unit or can easily pass information back and forth as needed. The chairperson must be the most committed person on your refugee resettlement team. Ideally, this person sticks with the project from start to finish. Other players may come and go as the tasks change, but the chairperson has to be able to coordinate the movements and keep all others headed in the right direction. Your objective is to guide the entire resettlement process to a successful outcome.

This reminds me of a scene in the movie *Cool Runnings*. John Candy, as Irv Blitzer, is talking about the commitment of a bobsled driver in relation to his team. He says, "The driver has to work harder than anyone. He's the first to show up, and the last to leave. When his buddies are all out drinking beer, he's up in his room studying pictures of turns. You see, a driver must remain focused one hundred percent at all times. Not only is he responsible for knowing every inch of every course he races, he's also responsible for the lives of the other men in the sled. Now do you want that responsibility?" OK, refugee resettlement is not that serious, nor does it take that level of preparation or focus. Yet, everyone will look to you to keep the process moving to the ultimate, successful conclusion.

The following paragraphs describe various skills required of the chairperson or at least one of the chairpersons. To avoid confusing references to a chairperson or chairpersons, the references below will assume there is a single chairperson. However, keep in mind that these tasks can be shared. It's just important, in a shared role, that all skills be covered by at least one of the chairpersons.

The first priority skill for a chairperson is the ability to delegate tasks to members of the various teams. Without this ability, the chairperson would become a one-person resettlement team. We've seen this happen and it is not pretty. A one-person resettlement team is a recipe for frustration, for both the refugee family and the chairperson. Burnout would be likely and the chance of ever trying another resettlement project is next to nothing. Delegation is an absolute must.

Organizational skills are important too, though you can compensate through good delegation to other organized individuals. There are many details to track throughout the resettlement process, so the ability to keep things straight will be a great help to your team.

As happens in any group, the participants will look to the leader for some level of expertise. In the resettlement process, at least initially, the chairperson will be viewed as the leader, even from the refugees' perspective. Therefore, it is advisable to have a chairperson with cross-cultural sensitivity. Actions and decisions made by refugees do not always fall in line with typical American thought processes. Someone who is tolerant of new ideas and different ways of thinking will be able to stay focused on the resettlement tasks without feeling challenged at every turn.

Related to the sensitivity just described are patience and flexibility. These attributes are not just necessary when dealing with the refugees, but also when dealing with our own bureaucracies and systems, and from time to time, the other members of the resettlement team. Whereas organizational skills are important, they cannot be too rigid. Not everything will work as planned.

A joyful disposition is also helpful. Sometimes things go wrong, refugees are confused, communication breaks down, team members get crossed up, and schedules collide. Have a sense of humor and laugh about the problems. Refugee resettlement is an important function with great and small rewards. You will miss those rewards if you only focus on the things that go wrong.

Now that you have an understanding of the skills, it's time to look at the tasks that the chairperson will perform.

The first thing you will likely do is sign a commitment form on behalf of your resettlement team. If you are working with Lutheran Social Services (LSS), you will sign a co-sponsorship commitment form on behalf of your congregation. The other designated resettlement agencies are likely to have a similar agreement. Having signed the appropriate commitment form you become the main point of contact between your resettlement team and the sponsoring organization.

Next, it's time to put together your refugee resettlement team if you haven't already. Find those people that will be interested and committed to the resettlement activities. Tell them to read this book to get an understanding of the different roles involved and determine where they would like to fit in.

Divide your committee members into appropriate teams. It's important for the chairperson to be involved, but to also allow others to take leadership of the teams they are involved in. The chairperson should not micromanage every detail. This will help you maintain your sanity and let others have some fun too.

With your full committee and a variety of teams assigned, you will need to schedule and lead regular meetings. At first, since there will be much to report, you may want weekly meetings. As the refugees start to settle in, less frequent gatherings will be sufficient, though ongoing communication will always be important.

Besides face-to-face meetings, you will need other ways to communicate with your resettlement team. We have found that subscribing to a list server so that all team members can keep each other informed works very well. Members can send a single message to the list. That message is distributed to all subscribed members of the group. Yahoo Groups, groups.yahoo.com, is a free online service that allows custom groups to communicate well. The only requirement is that each user has to create a login. Google also offers a similar shared calendar option, www.google. com/calendar. Shared online calendars can also help keep activities organized and reduce the chance of multiple appointments set for the same time. To keep up with options be sure to check in at the Refugee Resettlement Support blog, www.resettlementsupport.com.

One of your primary tasks is to work with all the teams as the resettlement project progresses to ensure that they perform all tasks in a timely manner. If the assigned persons are unable to complete their tasks, find others to help. If you have put together a good team, with a few alternates, you won't have to take over for anyone who drops out, just plug someone else into the appropriate role.

Someone must meet the refugees at the airport upon their arrival. Since the chairperson will likely be the most consistent participant in their lives, why not start from the moment they land? The lives of these people are in your hands; show them how much you care right away. If you cannot be at the airport, find someone who can. It is important that they see they are not alone in this strange place we call home. And, whoever goes to the airport should take a family picture! Someday you'll enjoy looking back on this moment.

Whoever meets the refugees at the airport should be aware that it's no longer possible to wait at the gate while passengers deplane. Now our closest approach is the end of the concourse outside the security checkpoint. At this vantage point, passengers from various flights might be mixed so, short of asking each person, there is no way to match people with flights. Therefore, depending on your airport and the appearance of your local and tourist population versus that of your incoming refugee family, you may or may not have difficulties spotting the refugees.

In any case, there is one telltale sign of refugees. They are carrying a white plastic IOM bag. This bag, issued by the International Organization of Migration, carries a number of important documents. On the side of the bag, in large letters, it says IOM. They have been instructed to carry this with them and keep it safe. Your task then is to watch for people who look confused by their surroundings, represent the ethnicity you suspect, and are carrying the IOM bag.

To help the refugees spot you, carry a welcome sign with their family name printed on it.

In case there happen to be several refugee families arriving at one time, be sure to verify family name, family members, and case number with your expectations. It can be awkward to pick up the wrong family leaving your family and another sponsor wondering what's going on!

Put together a phone list of everyone on your resettlement committee. You will be giving this to the refugee family as a reference. To help the family know who is who, I recommend you include a photo of each committee member next to their phone number. This way the family does not have to remember a name to know whom they want to call. After picking up the family at the airport, but before leaving them alone for their first night, give this list to the head of the family. Be sure to point out your own name and number when you hand over the list.

Be ready to participate or sit through an orientation for the refugees. You do not have to prepare the orientation, as the sponsoring agency must do this soon after the family's arrival, often, but not always, the same day. The agency will usually arrange for an interpreter. Since you won't always have that convenience, this is an opportunity, as the chairperson, to get answers to your questions. When you first met at the airport, you and the refugees might not have been able to understand each other fully. This orientation meeting may be your chance to be sure some things are said and understood.

While your housing team will take care of the details, you should double-check that all housing requirements are met. You should also be available during the housing inspection performed by someone from the sponsoring agency. Usually within 24 hours of arrival, the agency will verify that your team has provided for the refugees' basic needs. Therefore, you must be certain to have delivered all of the required items mentioned in the following sections. Failure to make all proper arrangements could result in the rapid end of your resettlement duties.

Track the time, mileage, and expenses of all of your resettlement team volunteers. This is good information to look back on when you consider helping another family. The information may also be required by your sponsoring agency; especially if it helps the refugees qualify for some financial assistance. It is likely that your agency may participate in the Federal Matching Grant Program. If so, this is a good thing, and you need to be aware of it. This has an impact on your employment and finance teams as well, so be sure to share information with them.

The Matching Grant Program is a federal initiative, funded by ORR, designed to help refugees become self-sufficient quickly without having to rely on a state welfare program. Participation in the program is a choice for the family, discussed during their orientation. If they choose this route, they receive financial assistance, job search support, and English classes. In turn, your team is required to "match" at least half the grant funding value with cash, volunteer time, and in-kind donations.

While this grant helps the refugee family directly, it also helps encourage you to seek community support for the resettlement effort. As a benefit, it reduces some of the employment workload on your team since job search support is included. The downside is that the program is limited to 4 to 6 months, and you must keep and submit records of your contributions, time, and other donations.

We have helped families with the Matching Grant Program and without. If it were our choice, we'd take the matching grant program every time! While there are record-keeping requirements, it's still easier than dealing with a welfare system. And I believe it helps accelerate self-sufficiency for your refugee family.

To help your family further accelerate its potential for success, try to find an existing community of people of similar or compatible origins. Such communities may share common language and may be able to guide the newer arrivals over some of the hurdles they faced when they came to the United States. However, do not assume that your family wants to meet others from their home country. Due to potential ethnic conflicts, this could create unwanted stress. If it's possible, ask them before setting up this type of meeting. If it's not possible to ask, you could try making an introduction in a neutral location without disclosing where the new refugee family lives. This way they remain in control of who they choose to interact with.

Also, be sure you do not think of your refugee family as somehow being your possession. After you put so much time and effort into their resettlement and adjustment, you will likely feel quite connected to them.

However, you do not wish to create a codependency. For your own sanity, and their ultimate success, you must be able to let go and even encourage their separation.

Finally, you must celebrate the successes. Offer praise to each of the various team leaders and other volunteers for their efforts. They will already feel good about doing something great, but it is even more special when you notice and appreciate their hard work.

See Appendix B for a complete checklist of the skills and tasks required for each aspect of your resettlement team. For a look at details from an actual resettlement, refer to the bonus material available at www.10milliontol.com/extras. Here you'll find a case study of activities and actual expenses incurred over an eight-month period.

Housing Team

The housing team works hardest at the beginning of the resettlement process, but also has some responsibilities, though decreased, as time goes on. The primary goal of this team is to secure a suitable place for your refugee family to live.

If you are thinking about being on the housing team, you will need a few skills to help you get by in this role. First, you have to have a willingness to make many phone calls. Finding appropriate (both suitable and affordable) housing is not always easy, and you may have to call around. As you're making those phone calls, talk to the potential property owners in a friendly, open manner. Most landlords want to know who is moving into their properties. With a refugee family, you don't even know them, but you have to be ready to vouch for them. Explain the situation to help the property owner feel comfortable. You also need a sense of urgency. It is important to get housing. The day the family arrives, they have to have somewhere to live. Finally, you need decisiveness. If the right deal comes along you might have to grab it without full approval from a large committee.

When you talk to the property owner you should tell the story of refugee resettlement, how you are helping this family become self-sufficient. Most successful landlord relationships are formed when you share the story of what you and your committee are doing to help refugees. Be open and honest and assure the landlord that you will be covering the rent at first and helping the family write checks to pay rent on time. You do not want the property owner to think there is any unusual risk. In fact, since you have a team helping, the risk should be lower than taking on a normal renter. If the property owner starts putting up a lot of resistance then don't rent there. Thank the landlord for their time and give your phone number to call back in case of a change of heart. Eventually you will find a receptive property owner or even one who enthusiastically embraces your mission.

So what will you need to do on the housing team? You need to find a place, or places, if timing isn't quite right, for the refugee family to live, and arrange to establish a new home for them.

Prior to the family's arrival you will need to look for <u>affordable</u> housing. This may be a difficult task in some communities, but keep in mind that your refugee family will have modest income at best, probably not much more than minimum wage to begin. Since the goal of resettlement is to help the family become self-sufficient, you will want to make sure that they move into housing that they can afford. You do not want your group burdened with paying rent any longer than necessary.

It's also important to look for <u>safe</u> housing. Refugee families have seen enough violence in their lives. Try to ensure they feel protected here. For them to move into a stage of productive, responsible, contributors in society, they will need to feel safer than they have in years.

Another important attribute is <u>convenient</u> housing. Many refugees have never driven a car. Even if they have, they will likely not be able to afford one for some time. We've received donations of automobiles from time to time, but there is still the cost of operation and insurance. Until they obtain a driver's license and they can afford the insurance, they may need access to public transportation. If bus service is available in your community, try to find housing that is near a bus stop. This will increase their mobility and self-sufficiency.

Also, look for <u>suitable</u> housing. With the biography of the family in hand, you should be able to determine the proper number of bedrooms needed. Parents should have their own room, though an infant can be in the same room. A boy can share a room with another boy, and a girl with another girl. A living room can be converted to a sleeping area if necessary. If the family is large, check to see if the property owner or local ordinances have certain living requirements. Odds are that you should get the smallest acceptable size apartment to keep it suitable for the family and yet affordable.

Arrange for occupancy of the housing. Because of the uncertain nature of refugee arrival, we recommend that you do not sign a lease until the family arrives, or at least not before the arrival is imminent. If this is troublesome, it can be beneficial to arrange for temporary housing initially. Then, when the family is in their first location, make final arrangements for their more permanent home. On several occasions, we have had refugee families live in part of our house for up to a couple weeks while other housing became available. This is a great experience for all involved.

You will have to prepare their home for arrival. While the Furniture Team and the Food and Clothing Teams verify that all the required items are available for the family, you will confirm that the accommodations are ready to receive the family and the donated items. Check that fire extinguishers are available. If none are provided with the housing, then purchase one or request one as a donation. Store the fire extinguisher in the kitchen and, after the family arrives, make sure they know how to use it!

After the family arrives, you must provide them with a way to make emergency phone calls. Since you will not likely have phone service installed prior to their arrival you may wish to provide them with a cell phone and a list of committee members' phone numbers along with police, fire, and ambulance numbers and/or 911. Another option is to show them the nearest pay phone and provide enough change to make a few calls. You may also need to show them how to use the phone.

At some point, your refugee family will receive some money as part of an initial resettlement grant. This money will come through the agency you are working with. But prior to that they may not have any cash.

Imagine yourself dropped in a foreign land with no local currency. Unless you're the really adventurous type, this won't sound like much fun. It is possible that the family will have arrived with some U.S. Dollars, but don't assume they did. Regardless, whether they came with some cash or with nothing, provide them with some "walking around money" to use for whatever they may need. With $25 per adult, they can buy some food in case they need something that you have not provided. Or, they can get on a bus, or do laundry. You don't know what they might need, and they might not be able to tell you. They might need something you would never provide, that you might think is completely illogical. That's OK. They might spend all of it at the first opportunity. They might not spend any, wanting to save for later. It's just important that they feel they can buy something if necessary. This little bit of money provides a little bit of freedom. They will appreciate that because freedom is probably something they have not had in quite some time.

Have utilities turned on in the name of the family. In most cases, the property owner will be paying any utilities until the new tenant moves in. Perhaps some of the utilities are included in rent. For any utilities that become the family's responsibility, you should notify the utility companies so that they can start billing properly and turn on service, if necessary. Even if your group decides to help cover utility costs at first, it is important for the family to start developing a credit record. By putting their name on all services, you help accomplish this.

Provide orientation to help the family understand the basics of their new home. Provide them with keys. Show how to lock and unlock the doors, turn on and off lights, heat and air conditioning. Explain everything in the kitchen: oven, stove, refrigerator, freezer, microwave oven, exhaust fans, etc. Point out the smoke detectors and test each one in front of them so they know the sound. Show them the bathroom, how to flush the toilet and turn on the bath and shower. Show them that they can flush toilet paper. Show them where to put garbage so that it can be hauled away.

Show the family how to do their laundry. If the apartment has machines that require coins to use, provide them some quarters and demonstrate the process. If your group provided a washer and dryer, make sure they know how to use them. If the family has to rely on a laundromat, show how to get there and how to use the machines. If the family decides to wash their clothes in the sink and hang them to dry, that's OK too. They may have never used a washing machine before so give it time.

Order telephone service. This can be difficult since the family has no credit history and no social security numbers upon arrival. You may have to wait until social security numbers are issued before you can order the service. That is typical. If you're comfortable with the idea, you could arrange for service in your own name at their location. Once they have social security numbers, switch the name on the service. If you're not comfortable with that idea, just have them follow the normal process, waiting as needed. It can be a good lesson for them to understand that not everything is going to go smoothly or happen in the time frame that they may desire. If the time drags on for weeks into months, be aware that the family will continue to ask you about phone service. Another option is to start the family with a mobile phone, skipping the entire landline process. While the cost may be a bit higher, the convenience and ease of getting started may be worth it. Though we have not used this option, I have heard that T-Mobile has worked well with refugees and that they offer some flexibility without first having social security numbers.

One more consideration with regard to phone service is to guarantee that 911 access is available. It is important that the family can get this emergency service immediately, from the day they move into their apartment. Also, you must verify that they understand how to call 911 in case of an emergency, and only in an emergency. If they are unable to get any form of telephone service right away, provide them with your own cell phone or even a cell phone that no longer has a service plan. A cell phone without an active service plan can call 911 as long as the phone is charged and turned on. If a cell phone is the only way to reach emergency help, teach the family how to repeat their address so that help knows where to find them.

From time to time, every home needs a little maintenance work. A nice gift to provide the family upon arrival is a basic set of tools. A hammer and screwdrivers, along with an assortment of nails and screws, are essential. A flashlight and some pliers can be nice additions. Not only does this have direct benefit for the family, but when anyone visits at a future date, and the family points out a problem, they will have access to tools right away.

For your refugee family, the concept of renter's insurance is probably completely foreign. At this point, I would recommend keeping it that way. Renter's insurance is important at the right time. But, like any insurance it is meant to insure assets. When a new refugee family arrives, they have very few assets. The things they are given are nice gifts, but they are generally used items that could easily be replaced if needed. Therefore, insurance is not necessary. Once the families get settled in, have jobs, and start acquiring their own things, then it may be good to start talking about renter's insurance. The exception to this is if the landlord requires the tenants to carry the insurance. Don't do anything that violates the property owner's trust. In that case, just get the least coverage, lowest cost available policy.

One final thought. It is helpful to both the refugee family and the property owner if you are an intermediary for some time. If there are problems, or perceived problems, have the family contact you or someone on your team. If the matter is not significant, help the family to resolve it on their own. This helps them with problem solving in their new life. The next step would be to see if someone on your team, or the larger resettlement committee, could help resolve the problem directly. For example, if there are minor plumbing issues, or the smoke detector needs new batteries, or a small area needs to be painted, just take care of the issue while the family watches. There is no need to get the landlord involved. Of course, if there is a serious issue, you can show the family how to contact the property owner, and you might even want to be present if the landlord has to show up. Both your refugee family and the landlord will be more comfortable with your presence.

Furnishings Team

The furnishings team is a short-term team, working hard at the beginning of the resettlement process. Its purpose is to make sure the refugees' home is appropriately furnished. Once the refugees' home is filled with all the required items, this group can disband.

The skills you will need include organization and coordination. You will need to organize a list of needs, coordinate with donors for the items, arrange for delivery, and track the items delivered, following up for those items that don't make it.

To begin, put together a complete list of furnishings and household items required for the size family you are receiving. For some items, you will need one per family. For other items, you will need one per person. Determine the total list in advance. The agency you are working with should provide you with a basic list. In fact, when you agree to work with an agency you will likely receive that list and be obligated to meet the minimum requirements.

Next, look for volunteers to provide the needed items. We have always placed a sign-up poster at church to solicit donations. We itemize each individual object. We provide space for a contact name and phone number. At a glance, we can tell what items have not yet been covered. Friends, family, and other people in your community can also be a good source for donations. Often people have things stored in their basement or garage that they would be willing to donate to free up their personal space. With nearly every resettlement, we've found one or more families in the process of moving, or clearing out an estate, that was willing to donate many items.

Arrange to get the furnishings to the refugees' new home. We have enjoyed the concept of "move-in day." We set up a date and time that we will fully furnish the home and ask all who can participate to bring their donated items. For those who cannot be available on move-in day or those with large items, we arrange pick-up either that day or in advance. If your refugee family can be part of the move-in day process, they gain perspective that their home is provided by volunteers who want to help them and that it is not mysteriously provided by the government or some other organization. They also feel pride in helping to put together their own new home.

Keep track of all items as they are delivered. Cross the items received off the master list. This way you will know if anything is missing. Place calls to the appropriate party to arrange for delivery or pick-up.

Watch for any extra needs and arrange to resolve them. Often when you are setting up a new home, you will become aware of a need that no one identified in advance. For example, on several occasions we have found that the apartment did not have any overhead lights. We received lamps among the donated items, but the lamps did not include light bulbs. Here's a need that we had to fill to prevent the family from living in the dark. Generally, we send someone to a local store before the move-in day ends to pick up the important extra items. For other things that come up that are not urgently needed, put together a new list, and post it back at church.

Let's go back to the required list of furnishings and household items. The basic list is provided because you and the sponsoring agency must meet the obligations to the U.S. State Department. This list protects the refugees from substandard living conditions, helping to ensure that they are not being dumped into an undesirable situation in a new country. In the following paragraphs, I'll go over each of the items you will find on that list. You can also find a complete checklist of each required item in Appendix B under the furnishings team. For each item, you may want to check with your agency as to whether there are any requirements for new, or if used items are acceptable.

First, each member of the family must have appropriate bedding. That's one complete bed (frame, box spring, and mattress) for each member of the family. A mattress on the floor is not acceptable bedding. Small children of the same sex and married couples may share a double bed. Whether the family chooses to use all the beds you provide is their decision. You have to provide them, but they don't have to use them. One of the families we sponsored started out with the mother and five children all sharing a pullout couch. This was a matter of their feeling comfortable in their environment. Not feeling secure, they also put a piece of furniture to block the apartment door at night. Over time, they relaxed as the traumas of the past became more distant.

The family must have a place to store their clothing. At a minimum, one set of drawers is required. You can strive for one dresser per person, but the requirement is one per family. Ideally, aim for one set of drawers per bedroom. This is generally enough to keep clothing put away, but not too many that you'll crowd out the space of a small apartment bedroom.

It is important that the entire family is able to sit down together at meal times. Whether they practice this is irrelevant at this point. You must provide a kitchen table along with one chair for each member of the family. The chairs and the table do not have to be a coordinated set. It's just important that every member of the family is able to sit at the kitchen table at one time.

The kitchen table is not the only place for a family to enjoy some time sitting together. Living room seating is required for each member of the family. A matching sofa and love seat is not necessary, but you must have enough seating so that every family member can sit, off the floor, at one time. A sofa or two can cover a lot of seating. (A sofa-sleeper can even count as one of the required beds so it can help meet seating and sleeping requirements.) There will be times that your refugee family would like to entertain guests so extra seating may be convenient if room and donations permit.

Another consideration is appropriate lighting in each room. If the apartment has overhead lights then you need to do nothing more than make sure they are working. Otherwise, provide at least one lamp for each room.

Finally, if the family has an infant, supply appropriate items for sleeping, sitting, and eating.

Let's talk specifically about kitchen requirements. The kitchen must have a working stove, oven, and refrigerator. Ideally find an apartment that includes these appliances. A microwave oven can be a nice convenience. Depending on where your refugees are from they may not have a concept of a microwave oven so training may be necessary. But, don't think that everyone knows about using a stove, oven, or refrigerator either. Assume they don't know. Show them how to use each appliance. You might have to repeat this exercise on more than one occasion. A freezer may also be something completely new to them.

One of our refugee families insisted they were familiar with stoves, so we skipped teaching this point. It turns out they had only used a slow-to-heat propane burner in the past. They now had an electric stove. One of the first times they made eggs in their new apartment, they put some oil in a pan, added the eggs, turned the burner on high, and then walked away thinking it would take some time to heat up. A minor fire emergency followed! This resulted in unplanned volunteer hours to repair and repaint the kitchen. The lesson is that you should go over everything.

In addition, be sure to provide the required fire extinguisher—it might be needed. (Note that a fire extinguisher is not required if the housing has overhead sprinklers, but it's still a good idea to have one.)

The family needs to be able to cook and prepare meals so you'll have to provide at least one saucepan, one frying pan, and one baking dish. Provide a set of mixing/serving bowls, and a set of cooking and serving utensils. To be ready to eat, provide at least one place setting including fork, spoon, knife, plate, bowl, and cup for each member of the family.

We have the convenience of being able to buy canned food at the grocery store, so they will likely need a can opener at some point. This is a required item.

For linens, the family will need one bath towel for each person, one set of sheets and blankets for each bed, and one pillow and one pillowcase for each person. Also, if you live in an environment that is colder than where your refugee family is from you might want to provide extra blankets. If they are moving from a hot region and you are in the northern U.S., they might enjoy even more blankets for the winter months.

You must provide the ability for the family to continue to live in a clean environment. This means that some cleaning supplies are necessary. Start them off with some dish soap, bathroom and kitchen cleanser, cleaning cloths and/or sponges, laundry detergent, at least two wastebaskets, a broom and/or mop, and a trash can or bags.

To maintain a clean body, you must provide some toilet paper, shampoo, soap (deodorant soap may be a good idea), one toothbrush for each person, and other personal hygiene items as appropriate for age and sex of family members.

Finally, there are a few miscellaneous things that will just help them get along better. An alarm clock is necessary, as you will discover when they need to be ready and waiting for you with appointments. They will need paper, pens/pencils, and scissors. Finally, check with the housing team to make sure the family received some spending money. Depending on how the move-in process went, your team may be in a better position to give them a little cash.

The items listed above are the minimum requirements of the U.S. Department of State. You may go above and beyond these requirements, but do not fall short. By taking on a refugee family, you are obligated to provide them with a certain minimum living standard. If your family feels they do not need or want any of the required items, they will have to sign an official statement to that effect. We would request the appropriate form through LSS. Likewise, whatever sponsoring agency you work through should provide that form or other instructions to follow.

The task of finding the required furnishings should take place prior to your refugee family's arrival. Once they arrive in their new home, all of the required items are necessary right away. They must have all items by the time of inspection, which may happen as soon as the family arrives at their housing or within 24 hours after arrival. If you are having difficulty finding any of the required items, contact your sponsoring agency to see if they can offer any assistance.

Food Team

The food team is a short-term team primarily responsible for stocking the kitchen for the first 30 days from the refugee family's arrival. It is also important to teach the family where and how to grocery shop.

This team begins its journey with a little research. You must learn about the culturally appropriate foods for your family. This is important because people of some cultures and religions will not eat certain things. If, for example, your refugee family will not consume pork, you shouldn't buy pork products. At a minimum that would be a silly mistake, but worse, it could be insulting. Your first task then will be to organize the donation of suitable dry and canned goods in advance of the family's arrival. You can acquire frozen foods once an apartment is secured. You should only purchase fresh goods after the family has arrived.

Upon the family's arrival, you will provide them with a hot meal. Depending on how far they have come, this might be their first real meal all day or even in several days. The meal should be nutritious and culturally appropriate. A casserole of familiar ingredients along with bread, fruit, and beverages may be sufficient. If others from the family's ethnic group are present in your community, they might be willing to help prepare some "comfort food." This lets your new refugee family know that you care and really starts the relationship off right. A relaxed atmosphere with good food can be very welcoming to strangers.

For this team you will need patience and tolerance as you work directly with the family to get foods that they need, or foods that are similar to what they need, or to explain that we don't have that here. You must also be willing to communicate knowing that your refugee family may understand little of your language. Some people can easily handle this, for others it is a terrible exercise.

Take them shopping the day after their arrival. Make this a trip for the whole family. Our grocery stores are probably much different from the stores of their home and certainly different from anything experienced in a refugee camp. Let them pick out items that are familiar to them. Be prepared to spend several hours at the store on the first trip.

At the same time, it is important that you have an understanding of the prices of various similar items and willingness to teach about brand name goods and off-brands. A family on a very limited budget may not be able to afford the same brands you normally buy. So teach about generic or store brands.

You will have to help them purchase fresh foods throughout the first 30 days. Also, some of the initial dry and canned goods will run low. When you plan to shop for replacements take the family, or at least the parents, with you. Each time, allow them more decisions in what they buy. You will learn about their desires and simultaneously be teaching them how to shop for themselves.

Although the financial obligation for your refugee resettlement team in regards to food is only 30 days, you might consider continuing to provide financial assistance longer if food stamps or similar programs are not available to them within that timeframe. Once the family has food stamps or income from a job, they can manage their own purchases. Your ongoing assistance will still help them shop wisely.

Be prepared to explain how frozen foods and other packaged items are stored and prepared. They may only have experience with fresh food or dry foods like rice. Many refugees have never seen a freezer so they are not familiar with storing food for later use. At the same time go over food safety issues such as putting leftovers in the refrigerator and how long is OK to keep fresh raw meat without freezing it.

Sometimes the family will express a desire for something unusual or very expensive. Sometimes this may be OK, but you should be teaching the family how to live effectively on a budget. Perhaps some other store has what they need for a better price. For example, several of the families we have worked with eat basmati rice as a staple. In most grocery stores, if they carry it at all, you can buy a small bag or container for several dollars. Warehouse clubs and local Indian or Asian grocery stores, if available, may offer 25 and 50-pound bags for only double or triple the price of a 1-pound bag. If you can find those deals, it becomes much easier for your refugee family to live and maintain some of their meal preferences.

While helping them to cook familiar foods is good, so is introducing them to American foods. They live here now and should at least become familiar with our diet (for better or worse depending on what study you may have recently read). Taking the family to McDonald's can also be a fun excursion. Odds are pretty good they have heard of McDonald's but have never seen one.

It is likely that your family will be interested in purchasing certain ethnic foods. We have great variety and it is likely possible to buy anything that they might want. Sometimes the price of certain things is well beyond reasonable. Be sure to explain the cost difference between buying at a specialty store or a convenience store and the pricing at one of the larger discount chains or warehouse stores.

Most refugees have never seen anything like the wide variety of goods we have in the U.S. and may be confused by the packaging, brand names, prices, weights, and preparation methods. Explain that store brands are comparable in quality with higher-priced name brand products. They also need to understand that store brands are only available at certain stores and different store brands are available at other stores. For this reason, it is a good habit to shop at a single grocery store if possible. Inevitably, the family will receive a donation of a gift card for a different store. If you take them to the other store, try to figure out the type of product they want and then find the related store brand. Also, try to teach the names of products rather than the brand name or coloring of packages. Roundy's flour or Sentry flour or Gold Medal flour are all flour regardless of how the packages appear. If the family understands "flour" then, eventually, they will be able to migrate to other stores without your assistance.

Most refugee families are able to take advantage of a food stamp program due to lack of income, at least at first. While I do not know if every state works this way, at least those I am aware of issues each family a card that is used like a debit card. The state makes a deposit once each month to their account. They can use the card to pay for food up to the remaining balance on the card. After completing the checkout process and paying for food, they will get a receipt that shows the remaining balance on the card. Since they are not spending cash, show them the value of what they spent and how much is available to spend before the next "refresh" date. This way, you can help them understand the impact of spending on their budget.

Keep in mind that non-food items may not be covered on their food cards at all. Just because they use it at a grocery store does not mean that they can purchase non-grocery products, even necessities. You should explain that using the card for food is correct, but that they should carry cash for soap, toothpaste, toilet paper, etc.

Typically, we have found that most families overspend during their first few weeks. In part, this is due to buying things that take some time to use up—bottles of oil, large bags of rice, flour and sugar—for example. In part, it is due to the availability of food unlike anything in their recent past. In part, it is due to their lack of understanding of the prices of the goods they are buying. Imagine you are in a foreign grocery store and are not fluent in the language. Will you buy the chicken soup that simply says "Chicken Soup" or the one that has fancy packaging with a tasty picture too? Which one costs more? If they pick up the one they understand, they may end up spending more money.

One other consideration for their overspending is the purchase of a lot of sugared beverages and snacks. You might feel they should spend their money more wisely. You are right to feel that way, but allow them the privilege at first. While getting used to a new diet of foods they may enjoy some familiar sweet goods and drinks. There is time to teach them about their spending habits after they settle in and start to get used to their new life. They may also use these items to welcome guests into their homes, having some snacks to fulfill their need to be hospitable.

While handling currency is not a primary responsibility of the food team, this is one area where the family will be spending money on a regular basis. It can be helpful if you are willing to teach and quiz their knowledge of American currency. The better their understanding, the sooner the food team can disband.

In several cases, we have had refugee families want to thank us for helping them. They use food as a gift of appreciation. It is not unusual for them to take some food item they have just purchased and give it to you. It is OK to accept a small gesture of thanks. Just try to clarify that it is truly a gift and not just a question of "what is this" or "what do I do with this?" Typically, the items given as gifts are things they already recognize and are often sweets.

Clothing Team

The clothing team is generally a short-term team, but can have some ongoing responsibilities. Since many refugees travel very light, they might only have one set of clothes, or, at best, enough for a couple days.

Your main task will be to provide adequate clothing for all occasions, including work, school, and everyday use. Pay special attention to make sure that each family member has appropriate footwear. Also, note that work and school may require additional footwear or uniforms. You will also have to keep in mind the season of the family's arrival.

If the family arrives during the summer, they will need appropriate winter clothes. In northern, snowy areas, give each member of the family a hat, gloves or mittens, boots, and a winter jacket. It may be best to provide these things at a seasonally appropriate time rather than dumping four seasons of clothing at once. If they came from a hot climate, they will not appreciate heavy winter jackets until they need to wear them.

Besides being seasonally appropriate, the clothing provided should be culturally appropriate. Some ethnic groups will not be comfortable wearing some typical American clothing. They may want help finding things that are more typical for their homeland. If you can accommodate their needs, they will feel more comfortable and cared for. This may help them remove an area of stress and help them adjust better. On the other hand, do not push their cultural dress if they want to look the part of a typical American. Blending in might be exactly what they want to achieve. You will have to take cues from the family.

If your refugee family has children under the age of two be sure to provide diapers. Cloth or disposable are acceptable.

To accomplish these tasks you will need a willingness to shop with little common language. That can require quite a bit of patience. You will also need the ability to say "no" when asked for unnecessary goods. As a sponsor, it is not your responsibility to purchase everything they might want. You need to provide what they need. Beyond that, if they desire something else, teach them to get a job, earn some money, and then they can buy whatever they would like.

The last thing to work on is to teach the family to use a washing machine and dryer to clean their clothes effectively. Some families may feel comfortable using a sink and hanging their clothes to dry. Teach them to use machines anyway. They might be overwhelmed at first but will catch on. Eventually they will enjoy the convenience. In addition, the machines do a better job of washing away cooking odors and body smells. That's a benefit sure to be appreciated by their American neighbors.

Medical Care Team

The medical care team ensures that all members of the refugee family receive any required and needed medical attention. At a minimum, this team will likely get each family member into the doctor's office for a general check up. If there are serious issues, this team will have more demands trying to provide appropriate care for each family member. Medical care providers have access to a language line on the telephone that can put them in touch with interpreters that speak a variety of languages. This way the doctors can communicate and the patient can understand. This alleviates you from having to provide interpreters for medical procedures.

It is important for you to realize at the beginning that you may learn some privileged information regarding your refugee family's health. For this reason it is likely that before you even get started you may be required to sign HIPAA confidentiality forms.

Confidentiality is a big issue in the medical community. As a co-sponsor, it is important that you also pay strict attention to protecting the confidentiality of your refugee family members. HIPAA is a federally regulated privacy policy stating that an individual has the right to disclose their medical information to whomever they choose. It is likely that you will not even be able to communicate the essence of HIPAA regulations to your refugee family. They will trust that you are working for them in their best interest. Treat their medical conditions with respect.

It may be ideal to have the medical team be a single person to limit the contact with the family's medical information. In reality though, a team of one can be too much of a burden on that person. It remains good advice to try to keep the medical team as small as reasonably possible. In some cases, it is possible that a refugee family will want complete privacy, not wishing to disclose medical conditions to you or your team. This is their right. You must respect that wish if you are in this position. In this case, the team's role becomes, more or less, transportation to medical appointments and little else.

If you are in a larger community, you may have to contact the public health department to see if there are any necessary health screenings. First, check with your sponsoring agency to see if they take care of this. You might be off the hook. However, if this is your team's responsibility, some common screenings may include:

- Health history
- Evaluation of immunization status
- TB (tuberculosis) test
- Chest x-rays
- Lead poisoning tests for children
- Testing for sexually transmitted diseases
- Blood testing for anemia (hematocrit)
- Hepatitis panel
- Pregnancy test

In smaller communities, testing may be limited to TB. In that case, it is important that a private physician perform a more complex exam.

After the family members complete any exams or screenings, be sure they follow up with the recommendations, which may include immunizations, medicines, or other actions. Try to help the family understand any prescribed treatments. In some cases, this may mean daily visits to the family to verify they are following the treatments or to help them do what is needed. In one of our refugee families, the mother had several teeth pulled in just a few weeks. She received antibiotics and painkillers, each with specific instructions. A member of our medical care team created a calendar starting with the day she began taking the medicines. The time of day to take the antibiotic was marked in red and the painkiller marked in blue. Then she marked the bottles with the corresponding color. Creative communication like this makes a tough situation much easier on everyone.

Every refugee arrives with some form of medical insurance for 8 months. Most often, they have Title 19 from the date they land in the U.S. Both for the sake of the family's health, and for ease of processing medical bills, try to handle as many medical issues as possible within the first 30 days of their arrival. After this time, they may be moved from Title 19 to a state or local health insurance coverage that may restrict the number of doctors available to service their needs.

Sometimes emergencies arise before the official medical cards arrive. The medical cards provide the required insurance information to medical care providers. Without them, there can be some confusion. To smooth things over under these conditions, have someone on the medical care team provide their own address as a billing contact to the doctor's or emergency room staff. When the bills arrive, just hold on to them. Do not pay them. Your resettlement team is not required to spend any money on medical care for the family. Just hold onto the bills until the medical insurance cards arrive. As soon as the cards arrive, call the appropriate billing departments to settle the payment. The insurance is retroactive to their first day in the country so this will not be a problem.

Schedule dental appointments as soon as possible. In some communities, dental options are limited depending on the type of dental coverage provided with their refugee insurance. Due to the lifestyle of many refugees in the time preceding their arrival in the U.S., dental needs are evident. The sooner these are resolved, the better. Don't be surprised if tooth extractions are necessary for several family members.

A more difficult issue to deal with is mental health. Post-traumatic stress syndrome is not uncommon among refugees. Sometimes it can be mild, sometimes quite severe. This is not a problem you have to work through on your own. If you notice symptoms, contact your sponsoring agency. They ought to be able to make an appropriate referral to mental health professionals in your community. Be careful about using the words "mental health" with your refugee family however. Depending on their culture, such a thought might be quite insulting. It's best to turn the whole matter over to your agency so you can stay out of it, except for possibly providing transportation.

Once any family members are employed, they may become eligible for health insurance through their employer. Help them take a health insurance option that works best for their situation. They are probably completely unfamiliar with the concept of medical insurance so your advice will be necessary for good decision-making. Medical insurance is likely an expense they have not considered, but it is usually a good idea that they take the insurance for their family, or at least the employed individual.

Employment Team

Employment is the primary goal toward self-sufficiency. The employment team can be one of the toughest teams. Therefore, it is vitally important to have more than one person in this group. This team prepares all employable adults (age 18-64, except women with infants under age one) for work and helping to look into job possibilities. It is also important that you are available to act as liaison between the refugees and their employers.

Before I get into details of the employment team, I would like to point out the importance of coordinating the job search with your sponsoring agency. Many of the agencies will hold onto at least some of the responsibility for finding employment, at least for the most employable member of the refugee family. Regardless of whether the agency is set to do all employment work or share the load, it does help speed up the process if members of your team are involved in the job search. This is one of the cases where more eyes are better. Just be sure to communicate with the agency so you are not duplicating efforts. The goal is to speed up the employment process, but you don't want to repeat the exact same activity, such as scheduling two interviews at the same company.

As a member of the employment team, you should have some patience, perhaps lots of patience. Not only will you have to have potential lengthy and frequent discussions with your refugee family regarding the importance of work and the expectations of employers, but you may also have to deal with employers who may not immediately see or understand the importance of hiring someone with limited English ability.

The first thing you will have to do with your family is set some mental groundwork for employment. The employment team, finance team, chairperson, or someone who develops an early close relationship with the family can handle this important step. Do not skip this step! It is important that the family understand the importance of work and the urgency of getting a job. They also must be set up for success, not given a feeling of hopelessness.

To set this groundwork, begin by showing the family the cost of everything they will have to pay for on a monthly basis. This includes their rent, whatever utilities (gas, electric, water) are not included with their housing, food, eventual repayment of airfare, telephone service, medical bills, and miscellaneous things that they might want for themselves.

After you add up the expenses, show the income/benefit side of the equation. Their current benefits include anything provided by the state for their survival. This may be food stamps, financial assistance like welfare, and medical assistance. Perhaps there is even some kind of housing allowance in your area. Generally, if you add these all up, they will not cover the expenses you established in the step above. Point out that the benefits fall short of what they need.

Then show how much money they will be able to make working a job. It's best to stick with a low hourly wage so that you don't set expectations too high. Sometimes a new refugee arrival will talk to someone who came earlier and learn about a higher paying job. This can be troublesome in that they may decide that they won't work for less than the other guy. This can be difficult to overcome, but is helped through this discussion. As of the writing of this book, minimum wage is $7.25 per hour. We use this as a starting number and demonstrate that at 40 hours per week, they will get $290 per week or about $1,250 per month. With a low-income family, income taxes will be negligible so we don't consider that in our calculations for this discussion.

Demonstrate that at this wage, working full time will cover their bills. Of course, we try to get a higher paying job and we try to get jobs for all potential family members. This helps assure them that they can do better and improve their situation by working hard. Also, show them that your resettlement team will help them cover costs while job-hunting. However, you are not helping them improve their situation or getting them things they might want. You are only helping them cover the minimum, the things they need.

By going through this process they understand early on that getting a job, even one of modest wage, will allow them to survive in this country. It is likely that the costs you show are beyond anything they could imagine, probably more money every month than they've ever earned in a year. Then you are following up by showing that they will also be earning more income than they've ever thought possible.

After the family understands the importance of employment, you can move on to other necessary steps in getting them a job. Start by interviewing the refugees to evaluate their skills and interests. With this information, you can write up simple resumes if needed. Visit various employers in the area and fill out job applications on their behalf. If the family has English-writing skills, you can also show them how to fill out an application.

Keep in mind gender and age issues, understanding that your refugee family might have certain stereotypical job role expectations. For example, it may be important that the husband earns more money than his wife and that the father earns more than his son. This is not something you should judge at this point. Let them keep whatever elements of pride that they have left. In their country of origin, the husband/father may have been the only employed person in the family and he may have earned enough to provide well for his family.

Next, you will have to orient them to the American workplace. They must learn to be prompt, call the company when they are sick, and give ample notice to their employer if they decide to move on to a different job. You may also have to show them proper work dress code and hygiene. Regarding hygiene, see the "difficult topics" section in a later chapter.

When, at last, one of the refugees is granted an interview, arrange to take them. Even if an interpreter is available, try to remain in the interview if the situation permits. Your presence can help give the employer additional confidence in their potential candidate, since you may be able to answer questions based on your relationship with the refugee family. You are also able to reassure the employer that your sponsorship team will help the new employee understand the job and its requirements. You may also be a friendly English-speaking contact that the employer can work through for a while.

Once the good news of a job offer comes, you'll likely have to help figure out transportation to the job. This may be teaching public transportation or arranging drivers to help them get to work. At this step, work with the Transportation Team to make sure needs are met going forward.

Finally, consider any children who would be left at home during the workday. There may be public childcare assistance available for families with low income. Head Start is often an option. You may also wish to work with the Education Team to help with this situation.

Education Team

Since employment is one of the primary goals toward self-sufficiency, education helps improve the employment situation for the adults and gets the children started on the right path. The initial goal for all family members is to learn English. While jobs without English speaking requirements exist, better jobs often require command of the language. For the children it is important to be enrolled in school. Your role on the education team is to help each member of the family get the appropriate level of education.

If possible, enroll adults in English language classes in your community. If that is not possible, find tutors who would be interested in teaching English as a second language. Or, best, do both. Start English classes as soon as possible. While getting a job normally takes some time, adults can get started with some basic English reading, writing, and speaking before they even start applying for jobs. To help make it easier for parents to get away for English study, you can provide childcare for any young children while the parents are away.

Enroll children in appropriate level schooling, whether daycare, preschool, or public school. Many school districts offer English as a Second Language (ESL), English Language Learning (ELL), or English for Speakers of Other Languages (ESOL) classes so check on the availability of classes and transportation to such schools. These types of classes are the best option because the teachers will have some training in how to teach English to non-English speaking persons. Public school ESL-type classes may also provide tutoring in various subjects to help the students keep up with their education. For any children enrolled in school, you should provide any required basic school supplies, at least the first year.

It can be great help for the children to have some tutors to assist with homework assignments. If your team members feel comfortable with this task, the family will readily accept the help. You can get outside tutors as well, preferably those who are willing to volunteer for this role. Sometimes you may need other outside assistance to cover more than just homework.

Children may bring home notes from the school or from their teachers. Even the adults may bring home information from their English classes. Help them understand this information. On the other side of the coin, be an advocate for the family with teachers and school officials. It makes their job easier if they know they can contact you with any issues.

Throughout the year, there may be a variety of school activities available for children and their families. Encourage the family to be involved, both at school and in the community. This helps strengthen their ties, expand their support system, and improve their independence.

As you work with your family for their education, you may uncover some interesting cultural issues. Share this information with the rest of your resettlement committee. This can help create and foster mutual understanding.

Before you know it, their English will improve to a level that allows you to call them on the phone. Then when you need to set appointments you will no longer have to drive over to see them and write on their calendar, but rather you can pick up the phone and talk. When they have enough English to speak on the phone, you can have your own private celebration!

Transportation Team

The ability to move around is a key to independence. At first, your refugee family will be dependent upon your group to provide transportation. You will need to wean them of this dependency over time.

Your committee chairperson may be meeting the family at the airport upon their arrival. If the chairperson cannot do this, or if the number of people is beyond that which the chairperson can transport, then the transportation team should arrange to welcome the family and get them to their apartment or other initial housing.

After this consideration, the primary role for the transportation team will be to provide for, or otherwise arrange, transportation to various functions, including their visit to the social security office, medical appointments, English classes, school for children, job interviews, shopping, and the post office.

In the process of making sure the family gets where they need to be, when they need to be there, you should teach transportation laws such as the use of seat belts, infant/toddler seats, no children in front seats, etc. Also, be sure to provide infant/toddler seats, age or size appropriate, for each child.

Learn what side of the street people drive on in their country and the country they most recently lived in. If the driving comes from the British tradition of the left side of the street, teach them that it is different here. Teach them to look left, not just right before stepping off the curb. Unfortunately, there have been refugee fatalities in this country due to habits of taking action after looking the wrong way. Can you imagine someone living through oppressive conditions for years only to finally get freedom and then be hit by a car? This is tragic for a family that has already been put through too much. With a little training, this situation is completely avoidable.

To help the family become self-sufficient, you should teach them how to use public transportation if it's available in your community. There are several things to consider. Is exact change required or can they get change? Can they buy bus passes? Where do they catch the bus? How do they transfer? What bus routes are available? The first time they use a bus, it will be helpful if you accompany and demonstrate. They can do this with very little language ability. In a matter of a few hours, they will have a good understanding of the bus system. For an example bus training guideline, refer to the bonus materials at www.10milliontol. com/extras.

For children, show them how to use school buses if this is how they will get to school.

If bicycles would be useful and desired, solicit donations for used bikes or offer assistance in purchasing bikes. Teach safety rules, including the proper use of helmets.

Help those of appropriate age obtain a driver's license. While it may be legal to drive using an international driver's license for a period of time, this is a privilege for tourists, not for persons establishing permanent residency. When the time comes, you may want to help them purchase a car.

Explain automobile insurance needs before the purchase. Depending on ages, how long they've had their driver's license, and other factors, insurance can be prohibitively expensive. Make sure they understand and can pay the costs before they buy a car. Also, keep in mind that insurance will cost more if they do not yet have a state driver's license.

Finance Team

Another key area in the development of self-sufficiency is the understanding of finances. The better your refugee family understands this, the more likely they will integrate well into society. It is the purpose of this team to not only give the family a good understanding of handling money, but also to help with financial decisions at the onset. It is likely that you'll want more than one person on this team, one to handle the financial relations with the family and another to handle the books for your resettlement committee.

Refugee families come from all walks of life. Some may be highly educated. Some may have been business owners. Some may have come from families of significant means. Some may have been in poverty their entire lives. Some have never seen a bank. Many, regardless of background, have never written a check or used a credit card. Some may have used barter as their primary payment method. You will need to understand your refugee family to ascertain their financial development needs.

Your first task will be to make sure that your refugee resettlement effort has sufficient funds for an initial housing security deposit, rent, food, and some pocket money to give to the refugee family. Note that if the family receives some onetime resettlement grant money through a resettlement agency, you may designate a portion of that towards rent and security deposit. This can help reduce the burden on your group.

Once the family arrives, it is important to ensure that refugees have some money within reach. Give the leader of the housing team $25 per adult family member to pass along to the family when they first arrive. Some may come with money and not need a handout. Others may come with nothing at all. A gift of $25, made up of a ten, two fives, and five singles is enough to give a feeling of security and can, at the same time, become a first currency lesson. This isn't much money, but provides them some freedom. They can choose how they would like to spend the money, if they spend it at all.

You might want to test the family to see what they understand about U.S. currency. It may be necessary to teach the coins. It's more likely they've encountered the bills in the past, as U.S. currency tends to circulate all over the world. However, you should not assume they know the bills either.

Help your refugee family understand the expenses they are likely to see. Even though your group may be paying their bills initially, it is important they understand them. Therefore, you should involve them with every check you write for them. Eventually they will be taking over. It's easier for you to explain as you go, and for them to understand, if they get little bits at a time. They'll also start to understand the regularity of certain expenses.

Once they understand the expenses, you can more easily demonstrate the importance of getting a job. It is not likely that public assistance will fully cover their expenses. This creates an urgency to work. Since working has likely been denied of them in the past, most refugees are excited by the opportunity to work and earn a living. They don't want to be dependent, and usually they don't have a sense of entitlement. Of course, there can be exceptions to this, but by setting the right attitude and expectations up front, you can counter any such tendencies that may want to develop.

Help the family make realistic goals concerning income. While they may talk to others and dream of a $20 per hour job, it's just not likely that this will be the first opportunity to come along. Do the math to show that a low paying, though better than minimum wage, job like $7.50 or $8.00 per hour is enough to cover the expenses. If a spouse can work, or a child is old enough, this extra income can really help the family get their finances in order.

Help the family open a checking account. We usually use some of their onetime resettlement grant money to open the account. Having an established banking record, rather than just working in cash is important when they get to the point of wanting to buy a car. And, yes, they will eventually want to buy a car. If they've had a good history at the bank, odds are good they can get a small loan.

Once the checking account is established, teach them how to write checks and balance a checkbook. As you probably know, there are plenty of people who were born and raised in the U.S. that have difficulty balancing their checkbook. Perhaps you're one of them. If so, this can be an especially challenging task. Be sure to have someone on the finance team who is comfortable in this role. Your assistance and demonstration over several months will help. Your task will be easier if they get checks that have duplicates attached to help keep the record until the account is balanced. The duplicates can also serve as a model if you write a few checks. The family can refer back to the duplicate checks to see how you wrote the checks.

When you open the checking account, you may have the option of adding an ATM card. Debit cards can be useful, freeing up the need to carry much cash. You'll have to explain how they work and how to transfer those expenses into their checkbook balance just like when they write a check. Be sure to explain that some ATM machines charge extra fees. Those dollars can add up quickly especially for someone who has little money to begin with. It is best to use the debit card for store purchases that are not covered by the food card, and to get cash from a bank's ATM that doesn't charge fees. Also, be careful if the bank wants to provide a credit card. I would suggest you decline credit cards. Using a debit card and running out of money is bad, but using a credit card and running up debt at a high interest rate is worse.

You will need to help the family identify and understand bills that come in the mail, separating them from the junk mail. They will need to know what the bill is for, who they need to pay, how much to pay, and when it is due. Be sure to help them understand the importance of paying their bills on time. Just like the checking account is important for future banking needs, so is a clean credit history.

Tax hits everyone, even refugees. When the tax season comes around, make sure they are able to file income taxes. Perhaps someone in your group or church can assist in filling out the forms. It's usually pretty easy, at least the first year. Depending on the family and the job(s) obtained it is also quite possible that they may receive more in refund than what they paid in to the IRS. Depending on your state, you may have to file state income tax forms too.

Keep detailed and accurate records of contributions and expenditures. At a minimum, you'll want to understand how much money your group spent on behalf of the family. This is useful when you decide to repeat your efforts with a new family. In addition, your primary resettlement agency may require you to submit such information for their records. Moreover, it's even possible that there will be minimum contribution requirements necessary to receive funding, so be sure to ask about that with your supporting resettlement agency.

One last note, be sure to reimburse members of your resettlement committee for out-of-pocket expenses. Unless they specifically requested that their expense is a contribution to the family, pay them back out of your general working funds. Your committee members are already contributing significant time. You should assure them that they don't have to spend money too, unless they choose to.

Public Relations Team

This team is responsible for educating the people outside your core group about the importance of refugee resettlement. A good PR team can help raise awareness of your efforts and increase the donations—cash, goods, and volunteer time—that you receive for your resettlement project.

Your first task is to start generating outside interest in your resettlement project. Prepare fliers to pass out and/or posters to hang in strategic places.

If your resettlement committee is a church group, see if you can speak in church, put a poster up in the narthex or a hallway, or even solicit donations for the project. Likewise, if you are part of a community service club or other civic group, talk to the members, and even consider the larger organization body, trying to find others who are willing to donate to your endeavors.

Keep people informed of your refugee family's progress. People can be supportive when things are going well and when things are not so well. They just like to know how it's going. The biggest factor in maintaining positive support is the continuation of good communication.

Show gratitude. Send thank-you notes to those who have donated. We have always made custom thank-you cards that include a photo of the family along with their signatures. It's OK to scan their signatures and print from a computer to save time. Most people enjoy seeing the personalization, and foreign signatures are often very interesting to look at.

After the refugee family has settled in and have become less dependent upon your resettlement team, plan an event to introduce them to those who helped make their new life possible. It can be fun for people to meet the refugees, and it's a nice way for the refugees to say thank-you in person.

You may also discover that various media would like to interview you and/or your refugee family. This is more likely if this is the first time refugees have been resettled in your area, or if this is the first time someone from this particular ethnic group has arrived. You may wish to check with policies of whatever Volag you are working with. Some may require all media inquiries to go through them. If that is the case, they likely have professional staff that will assist with the media contact. Also, note that if the media approaches you directly, you still have the right to decline an interview or a photograph.

Now, having said that, working with media can be a very positive experience. Keep in mind that your role with the media is to focus conversation on your personal experience and the experience of your refugee family. It would be wise to avoid expressing your personal opinions of national or international resettlement policies. This would just serve to stir up emotions and divide the audience as to the efforts you are making.

Things that work well to share are stories about why or how you got involved with resettlement, what you have done to prepare for the arrival of a family, or how refugee resettlement makes you feel. In other words, you are sharing your reasons discussed in Chapter 2 about why resettle refugees. Some background information on the ethnic group you are serving and some specific stories from the family will help strengthen the report even more.

Expect feedback due to any media coverage. You are likely to discover new supporters as well as those who really don't understand the point and argue against resettlement. In the past, our media efforts have resulted in volunteer interpreters, other members of the appropriate ethnic community stepping forward to help or at least acknowledge their presence, and donations of cash and services. You may also encounter some people who complain that you should be using your charitable time in other ways.

At all times you must protect the confidentiality of your refugee family. It would not be good if someone opposed to immigration decided to take matters into their own hands, paying a visit to your refugee family at their address that somebody made public. You need to be the family's advocate, safeguarding both their privacy and their dignity.

CHAPTER 5

RESETTLEMENT TIME LINE

We weren't allowed to be citizens in our own country. Though we were born and raised here, the local population still believed us to be outsiders. As a whole population, we were moved to different parts of the country several times over periods of decades, continually rejected and discriminated against. We had no chance of living a normal life within the rules of society. Even the police would force their way into our homes to steal our televisions or other things of value. We're good hardworking people, if only we'd be given a chance. Finally, our entire population was classified as refugees and we were allowed to leave. Our future is much brighter now as we have control of our own destinies.

In the last chapter, we looked at all of the different teams you will need to make your resettlement project successful. This chapter takes a different perspective, trying to lay out tasks in the order they occur. This ordering gives a better idea of when your teams must accomplish certain tasks, suggests how tasks of different teams overlap in time, and exposes some activities that you may not have previously assigned.

Keep in mind that the times presented here are guidelines. Due to a variety of circumstances that will be unique to each resettlement, certain things may have to happen sooner, or later, than the ideal plan. Different Volags may also make different timeline recommendations based on their experience. It's even possible that a single agency will recommend different timing in various parts of the country. For example, you'll see below that I suggest a trip to the social security office as an arrival-day event. I have heard, in some areas, the local social security office will not have any information in their computer systems yet. Such a visit on day one would then be a frustrating waste of time. If this is your first resettlement, be sure to tap into the extensive knowledge already accumulated with the personnel at your supporting agency.

Regardless of whatever else is going on, there is one thing that you must not miss: ON ARRIVAL DAY, SOMEONE MUST MEET THE FAMILY AT THE AIRPORT! We've heard stories of families arriving and waiting in the airport for someone to pick them up and no one coming for them. This becomes a burden on airport staff and whoever must come in quickly to pick up the pieces. Imagine the feelings of the refugee family put in this position.

You can use the following list as an extra checklist to make sure someone addresses all of the most important activities. As an example of a previously unassigned task, you'll see in week one that there is a need to apply for available social services such as food and medical assistance. This task does not show up on a specific team's list. Does your resettlement agency take care of this item? If not, you could designate it as part of the food team or the medical team or, what we've usually done, is assign the task to the employment team. We've chosen the employment team simply because they don't have much to do in week one. The point is that you should go over the elements of this list in your regularly scheduled refugee team meetings, and assign someone to cover each activity.

In advance of refugee family arrival:
- Decide to sponsor a refugee family.
- Put together a list of committee members including names and contact information.

- Convene an orientation meeting of your entire resettlement team and anyone who may be interested in joining your team. Your sponsoring agency may conduct or participate in this meeting.
- Divide your team into the smaller working teams described in the previous chapter, allowing people to express their area(s) of interest.
- Housing, Furnishings, and PR teams should get started right away.
- Determine initial housing situation.
- Find and furnish housing if appropriate. Or, make arrangements for temporary housing.

Immediately prior to family arrival:
- Decide who will meet the family at the airport. Arrange enough space to transport family and luggage to their initial housing.
- Decide who will prepare a hot meal for the family to eat on arrival day.
- Decide who will work with the family on arrival day, or the day after, for their social security office visit.
- Fill out social security applications with known biography data.

Arrival day:
- Welcome the family at the airport.
- Complete social security application with assistance of refugee family. Coordinate with sponsoring agency as they might help with this.
- Take immediately to social security office if open.
- Deliver to initial housing.
- Feed a good meal.
- Give an opportunity to make a brief phone call home. A phone card is a convenient way to limit the potential cost.
- Allow for privacy and a good night sleep.

Day one/first business day:
- Apply for social security cards if not completed yesterday.
- Make appointment with local health department for TB tests and any required immunizations (again the agency may be involved with this).
- Make copies of I-94 form and any IOM documents. Keep a copy for your reference and for sponsoring agency caseworker.
- If lease paperwork is available, make a copy for yourself and caseworker.
- Take the family grocery shopping.

Week one:
- Complete a refugee orientation meeting with sponsoring agency caseworker.
- Apply for available social services such as food and medical assistance.
- Enroll adults in English as a Second Language (ESL) classes.
- Enroll children in school.
- Begin looking for jobs.
- Assess the clothing situation. Help them do laundry. Take the family clothing shopping if the quantities they brought are insufficient.

Weeks two to four:
- The social security card should finally arrive. Hold a victory celebration!
- Photocopy the SS card. Keep copy and send copy to sponsoring agency caseworker.
- Once SS card is in hand, apply for a state ID card.
- Initial shopping experiences may have been overwhelming. After the first couple weeks, start showing them how to comparison shop.
- Demonstrate how to save money with coupons and/or grocery store savings card.

- If they are receiving food stamps or comparable program, show how to use the program.
- If there are medical emergencies before medical cards arrive, have bills sent to someone on the medical team. Do not pay the bills until insurance arrives to cover it.
- As soon as Title 19 medical card arrives, make appointments for a general checkup for each family member.
- Make dental appointments for each family member as well.
- Open a checking account at a local bank.
- All males 18-25 must register for selective service.
- Teach how to ride the local bus.

Months two to four:
- Employment, employment, employment!
- During this time, you must try in earnest to get jobs for all adults.
- Fill out job applications and teach all adults how to do the same.
- Take them to job interviews. Be their advocate if you can.
- Arrange for childcare.
- If applicable, find part-time jobs for teenagers.
- (optional) Ask for volunteers from your committee, congregation, or community to tutor children and adults in English, and help with homework.
- Celebrate birthdays and holidays (their holidays and our holidays).
- Continue medical and dental appointments.
- Go over family budget and finances.
- Help sort through the mail – by now they are starting to get bills and junk mail.
- Teach check writing and paying bills.
- Concentrate on issues, questions, or behaviors that need to be resolved:
  - skipping school
  - hitting or fighting

- corporal punishment
- ritual or cultural bodily mutilation (FGM is illegal)
- not being ready for appointments
- not storing food properly
- how to be a good neighbor
- If energy assistance is available, apply – appointments may be seasonal.
- Be available for any sponsoring agency evaluation meetings (30, 60, and/or 90 days).
- Help adult(s) get driver's license.
- When employed, assign a person to be liaison between employee and employer.
  - Be responsible for turning in paperwork.
  - Teach refugee how to call in sick or take off work for appointments.
- Chairperson should determine if committee meetings are needed.

Months five and six:
- Organize a gathering between refugee family and committee or congregation.
- Depending on the time of year, if kids are on summer break, help them enroll in summer activities.
- Get library cards and teach them how to use library and library computers.
- Some government assistance programs may have 6-month reviews. Someone from the committee should go along.
- Keep on top of housing maintenance issues.
- Airfare repayment bills may begin to arrive. Make sure they know how to repay them.
- At this point, it's the opposite season from when they arrived. Check to see if appropriate new clothing is needed.
- Chairperson should determine if committee meetings remain necessary.

CHAPTER 6

THE SYSTEM

I lived in a refugee camp for nearly a year. The camp lacked good facilities, food, health care, and shelter. I was assigned a place in "barracks" made of bamboo with thatched roofs and walls.

There were many kinds of biting insects especially mosquitoes, and there were rats and snakes too. Many of the snakes were poisonous so I was often afraid. We had to chase them into the woods near the edge of the camp.

We were given very little to eat and had to buy extra food from the local people who came to the fence of the camp to sell their stuff to us. They sold food, cigarettes, marijuana, and alcohol. The alcohol caused many problems in the camp.

Living in the refugee camp was horrible. I would like to forget it, but know that I never will.

Dealing With "The System"

"The System," as it's often called, is often a frustrating labyrinth of entanglement, a swirling sucking eddy of despair, requiring an off-the-charts-IQ and the equivalent of a PhD to master its fine points.

Dealing with "the system," and the people in it, can be one of the greatest challenges in refugee resettlement. Its concepts can be more foreign than the prospect of communicating with someone who doesn't speak your language. Nevertheless, "the system" serves a purpose. Just grit your teeth, exercise some patience, and you'll do fine.

The I-94 Card

No, the I-94 card does not provide free transportation on the interstate highway from Michigan to Montana. Rather, this is the official designation of the alien registration card. This card is one of the keys that will help you succeed in your upcoming journey through "the system."

The I-94 card shows the date of arrival in the U.S., their name, birth date, refugee status, employment authorization, and an 8-digit number that stays with them until they become citizens. If you're lucky, the card will also include two passport-size photos of each individual, and the photos will be stapled or clipped to the card. Sometimes, however, there may only be a single family photo. It's also possible that you'll simply get a separate sheet of paper that is actually a photocopy of the real photos. Regardless of how it appears, the refugees will have to show this card, and the photos, often during the first few days after their arrival. They should carry the I-94 and all supporting papers at all times.

For you, it's a good idea to make copies of the I-94 cards. Keep the copies in a safe place. If an original is lost, it's easier to replace if a copy is available. Note that if you find any of the information on the I-94 card is incorrect, you can fix it by filing form I-102, preferably before applying for a social security number.

Social Security

Dealing with the Social Security office has never been easy. But, the need to get through the doors of the Social Security office is hurdle number one. Yet even when you do everything right, there might still be problems. Here's an actual situation that we discovered.

Our first refugee family arrived with five family members. We did not realize at the time, that when Social Security card applications were entered into the computer that the last name, first 5 letters of the first name, middle initial, and birth date were used to create a unique identifier for each individual. That seems pretty safe. The youngest children of this family were twins with similar names differing only on the sixth and final letter of their names. They did not have middle names. See the problem here? Their "unique" identifiers were identical. When the Social Security cards arrived, the twins received cards with identical numbers. It took three months to clear that up. In retrospect, we could have solved this problem by assigning middle initials to each child prior to applying. Who would have known that?

A Social Security card is necessary for employment. It's necessary for any public assistance. It's required for a bank account. It's even necessary to get telephone service. The sooner your refugees apply for a Social Security card, the sooner they are on their way to self-sufficiency. Therefore, if it is possible to get to the Social Security office between picking up your refugees at the airport and taking them to their new home, do it! It may seem like you're rushing into this and that it would be better for the family to get some rest. You and they will be much happier in the end if you take time the first day to do this. If they arrive on a weekend or after the office is closed, then make a Social Security trip your first event on the next business day.

To prepare, get applications in advance of the family's arrival. Complete all the information you already know from the family's biography. Upon their arrival, prior to going to the Social Security office, ask them for the information that is missing. Hopefully you have an interpreter with you at this point so that errors can be avoided.

Make a copy of the information provided on the application. If you can photocopy it prior to giving it to the Social Security office, that is ideal. If not, write the information down for future reference. In a year or so, the family will likely want to apply for their "Green Card." This application asks questions that were on the social security application. The answers provided on the "Green Card" application must match. For example, sometimes the spellings of parents' names or maiden names are only known in the original alphabet. Spelling in our alphabet is just a matter of writing down the sounds that we hear. That first spelling becomes official so use that same spelling in the future. Without saving a copy, you'll only be guessing how it was spelled the first time. Save a copy and you'll save some frustration down the road.

Everyone applying for a Social Security card must apply in person. They will need to have a completed and signed application form and their I-94 card. If they already have employment authorization cards, they should take these too. If they don't have employment authorization cards you will have to apply for these separately, having photos taken and completing the appropriate application. Finally, if they have one, they should take their passport. Once they have presented their forms of identity and application, they should get a written receipt indicating that they have applied. If you do not receive this automatically, request that you get a written confirmation. This could be useful later especially if problems arise.

Officially, Social Security cards are supposed to arrive within 2 weeks. We've seen much longer delays with averages being roughly 3 weeks to a month. The actual Social Security numbers, as opposed to the cards, are often available much sooner and can be obtained in person. Get the numbers as soon as they become available. While the card itself is necessary for some services, the number is sufficient to start working with public assistance and for opening a bank account.

State ID Card and Driver's License

These days it is nearly impossible to transact any form of business without one or more forms of identification. Therefore, every adult should obtain a state or county ID card. If they are eligible for a driver's license, this is the most preferred form of identification. However, a state ID card can often be obtained before all driver's license requirements are completed.

ID card application requirements may vary by state or county. Minimum requirements may include:

1. **Proof of name and date of birth through a certified birth certificate, passport, or naturalization papers.** The I-94 card satisfies this requirement.

2. **Acceptable proof of identity.** A social security card meets this requirement. A state issued medical assistance or food card will meet this requirement too. A foreign driver's license or passport <u>might</u> be accepted. Finding an acceptable proof of identity is the most difficult requirement to meet if the social security card is not available.

3. **Proof of state residency.** A letter from the refugee sponsoring agency and a piece of mail sent to them at their current address can meet this requirement.

4. **Social security number.** If the social security card is not available, just knowing the number is good enough for this requirement. An ID card cannot be obtained without knowing the social security number. The desire to have an ID card or driver's license is a good reason to apply for that social security card as soon as possible.

Standing in line at the Department of Motor Vehicles is rarely a good time. With this in mind, be prepared so that you can avoid having to repeat the exercise. As a hint, take every form of identification that the refugee family has with them. This could include their passports, driver's licenses, school ID cards, other photo identifications from their home or interim countries.

To check on the ID card requirements for your state, you might want to go to www.dmv.org/id-cards.php. For driver's licensing permit information, see www.dmv.org/drivers-permits.php. This website allows you to choose your state and provides links to the appropriate resources within your state government. The refugee agency you are working with can also provide you with information based on their experience.

The Bank

As soon as possible, you should open a checking account for the family. If there is a single parent, the account should be in his or her name. If there is a married couple, it should be a joint account in both names. All named persons must be present with at least two forms of identification each, one of which must be a photo ID.

If you have managed to get a social security card and state ID by this time, those two pieces are all that is necessary to open a bank account. If you don't have those documents, the process is more difficult, but not impossible. Each adult refugee comes to this country with the authorization to get a job. As such, they already have, or can easily obtain, an Employment Authorization card. The U.S. government issues this card. Since it contains a photo, it counts as a valid ID. The I-94 card is a separate ID that may or may not have a photo attached. This card can be used as a second ID.

Of course banks are independent businesses that can refuse to provide services if they wish. As an advocate for your refugee family, your goal in banking is to make the bank as comfortable as possible with their potential new customers. For this reason, I recommend taking every form of identification that your family has available. If they have a driver's license from their home country, take it. If they have a passport, take it. If they have received a bill at their new address, take it to prove residency. Start with the employment authorization and I-94 cards, but bring out the rest, allowing the bank to photocopy any that they feel will be useful. You may also offer your own name, address, and phone number as an additional contact. Having someone who can speak clear English to answer questions might be all the comfort factor needed.

So which bank, and what type of account should you get? For a bank, as much as possible, go to the bank that is nearest their home. Your refugee family may not have their own transportation for some time. If the bank is within easy walking distance, that is a strong plus. If such locale is not available, choose a bank that can be reached easily by bus. If this is not possible, then pick a bank that you are willing to drive them to on an as needed basis.

The bank account should be a checking account with a low minimum balance requirement. Some banks require a minimum amount to open an account, but then offer no minimum balance monthly. This is ideal as long as there are no service charges when the account is below a certain threshold. Since the employment picture is uncertain at this point, you do not want to set up the family in a situation where their money goes away without going toward a needed expense. The account that some banks call "free checking" might be the best option. While an interest-bearing account would be a nice bonus, it is not necessary.

For the opening balance, we take a portion of the grant money that the family receives and use that to open the account. This money belongs to the family. By opening the account with it, it becomes a catalyst for future bill paying, savings, and credit.

Upon opening an account, the bank will ask what type of checks they desire. Don't overwhelm your family with check choices. They probably do not understand much of this process anyway. You should choose "duplicate-checks" so that you can review each check written and help balance the checkbook. The duplicates can also be a guide for future check writing. In most cases, the bank will mail, or make available for pick-up, the blank checks within a week or two. In the meantime, they will likely provide some temporary checks. Local merchants may not accept these checks but they are good for paying utility bills. Once the "real" checks arrive, you can use the remaining temporary checks to create written templates for recurring payments. Be sure to VOID these checks so they are not actually used. Perhaps write VOID in the position where the name, address, and check number would appear on the real checks. This way it may be less confusing.

The Phone Company

The phone company is an organization with layers upon layers of bureaucracy specifically designed to cause turmoil and confusion. Well, maybe that is not literally true, but the feelings evoked while jumping through their hoops may certainly conjure that impression. Establishing phone service in the United States requires a credit history. Clearly, your refugee family has no such history in this country. Without a credit history, they must present their social security cards. The social security number is not sufficient. You will need to have their cards available. As we discussed earlier, the social security cards can take three weeks to a month or more to arrive. This means that you cannot follow normal processes to establish telephone service during that period.

This will be frustrating not only to you, but to your refugee family as well. Most likely, there is no clear way for you to explain why they can't have a phone for month. Each time you see them they will ask about the phone service. They will say they need phone service. As an infant learns to say "mama" as its first word, refugees often learn to say, "I need a phone" or "where's my phone?" Of course, when you finally come through with the phone hook-up you will be a hero.

Here's a story of one resettlement committee's successful process working with AT&T, talking to dozens of people over a period of a couple weeks. Persistence was the key. *"I started with someone at Customer Care 1-800-924-1000 who started the paperwork. They couldn't proceed, so sent me to National Credit Verification Center 1-800-870-9582. Someone there asked me to fax copies of their I-94 cards and pages from the passport detailing name, birthdate, etc. to 1-800-668-6613. She told me to allow 24-48 hours to process. After that, I was told they couldn't read something on the passport, so I had to fax it again. Once that was approved, only then was I told I would have to make a $50 deposit before they could proceed, which I did via Western Union on their recommendation. Then I had to call Customer Care again and practically start over with someone new, but this time we made more progress. Next I had to call the Credit Verification Center and ask them to send the approval over to Customer Care. Once they did that, my representative was able to actually give me a number and start service. It went more-or-less in that order."* Note that in this example service was obtained without social security cards.

By agreeing to help resettle refugees, you also agree to provide the family with the ability to make emergency phone calls from the moment they arrive. That means they have to be able to reach a telephone at any time. So you find housing, but you cannot install a phone yet. You've got to be creative. For example, is there a pay phone nearby? If so, provide a roll of quarters and show them how to use it. Can you provide them with someone's spare cell phone? Even an old cell phone without a service plan will make calls to 911 as long as the battery is charged. Would you be willing to install a telephone in your name? If so, would the phone company be willing to change the names on the account after the social security card is available? Can you provide the refugee family with a key to your home, or to the nearby home of someone else?

On the good side, if your refugee family is receiving any public assistance they are likely eligible for free telephone installation and discounted monthly service. Be sure to request these discounts when you call for installation. You may be required to complete and return an application. In most cases, the full charges, along with installation, will still appear on the first phone bill. Once the phone company verifies the application against public assistance records, they will issue a credit later. If you do not see a credit by the second bill, call to inquire on the status.

When initiating telephone service, start out by blocking the ability to make long distance calls. Also, block the receipt of collect calls. Many refugee families have gotten in deep financial trouble early on by running up huge phone bills calling their relatives back home and accepting their calls. Instead, consider providing the refugee family with phone calling cards for long distance calls. These cards can be a good donation suggestion for people who would like to help your resettlement efforts without being actively involved. Phone cards are beneficial in limiting expenses while teaching the costs of long distance calling. There are calling cards designed to offer extremely low rates to specific countries. If your refugee family is going to call their home country, look for cards with deep discounts to that country or region. Sometimes a $5 phone card can provide more than an hour of international calling. Compare that to potentially $3 per minute with the long distance service that comes default on their phone line. Calling cards make sense.

Before we leave the topic of phone service, note that providing an answering machine is very useful. Once phone service is established they will get phone calls, and they may not be comfortable answering the phone because of language difficulties. An answering machine allows them to save messages that someone else can listen to later. This way if a social service, doctor's office, or employer needs to communicate, you can listen to the message and take appropriate action. It also allows the family to play the message repeatedly, perhaps finding new words in a dictionary, to help understand the message without outside help.

Utilities

Most of the time working with the local utility companies will be easy. The family moves in, you notify the utility of a new resident at their address, the date they moved in, and billing starts.

However, sometimes things just don't make sense. For example, with one family we ran into the situation where we could not get the local electric utility to accept the identification of the father in our refugee family. The utility continued providing electricity, but they would not send a bill because they had not accepted the evidence that the family is real. They were concerned about the possibility of setting up a fraudulent account. The interesting thing is that they have adopted a flawed process. They might prevent a legitimate customer from being able to pay. Huh? If they send a bill to the address where they provide service, they might be paid. However, if they assume they're going to be cheated and never send a bill, they certainly won't be paid. Clearly, this is a poor choice of action. If this were the storyline in a movie, no one would believe it!

Now, go out another month, the utility is still not charging the family for electricity. We know that eventually things will be worked out so we applied for low-income energy assistance for the winter. Because the assistance agency could not access legitimate records with the power utility, they could not apply an assistance credit to the family's electric bill. Therefore, they offered to mail a check directly to the family. They apologized that the family would have to cash the check and continue to pay the full value of the energy bills. What? The utility is unwilling to accept money from someone who might not be real, but the agency is willing to give the same family money? Where has the system gone wrong?

I present this story because you need to understand that some things just won't make sense. You may learn the right way to proceed, but the people involved just don't get it. In this case, you're not dealing with refugees that are lost and confused, but rather employees within our own native systems and businesses. Be persistent, and things will work out.

Food and Medical Assistance

When the refugee families arrive, they will qualify for various social services including food and medical assistance. To get access to these services they will probably require an intake interview at the office of a designated state or local government agency in your area. Your sponsoring organization may initiate these services. If not, they can tell you how to get started.

Assuming your team helps with the application for food and medical benefits, plan to take all adult family members, and the identification of any children, to the intake interview. Be sure an interpreter is present. When you set an appointment, ask the intake agency if they provide interpreters or if you will need to find and bring one.

Throughout the interview, data will be collected that is used to determine the level of public assistance that will be provided to the family. It is important to complete the intake and application right away so that the refugee family's benefits start as soon as possible. In some cases, you may be able to start the application process online. Again, refer to your sponsoring organization for more details.

While refugees receive a guarantee of medical insurance from the date of their arrival, it will be easier for you if they have the proper documentation whenever you need to work with medical caregivers. As for food, since they don't arrive with any income they should qualify for food stamps or a comparable program. Most likely, the family will receive a government issued debit card, called EBT, that is credited monthly. Getting this food credit or allowance will help them become self-sufficient in their grocery shopping.

One thing that can become confusing is that food and medical assistance can, and should, go away over time. As the family enters the world of employment, their dependence upon public assistance is lessened. Still they may not understand why they might receive $400 of food allowances one month and then only $100 the next. At some point, their employment income may disqualify them completely. You and they must view this as a positive development. They earn enough money to handle their expenses on their own without government support.

Eventually, the employed family members may become eligible for insurance through their employers. With that eligibility, they are likely to lose access to the government provided insurance. While this is likely to be more costly, it is another step to their independence and their successful integration into our society. Explain their progress and celebrate it.

CHAPTER 7

COMMUNICATION

There was civil war raging in my country. My family had to keep moving, from one refugee camp to another. I got separated from my father and brother. I tried, but I could not find them. Sometimes when I asked, I could get news about my father from the Red Cross. He was often sick, going in and out of refugee camp hospitals. I could never learn what was wrong with him, just that he was ill.

Eventually my aunt and I were granted refugee status and we came to the United States. I never saw my father or brother again. Now I can only hope that someday we can be reunited here. Because of the war, life did not turn out the way I expected it to.

Nonjudgmental frame of mind

Refugees come from all different regions, races, ethnicities, religions, and socio-economic backgrounds. It is important not to judge them, or what they say, based solely on your world view. The lives and reactions of your refugee family may run counter to the way you normally think. It is important to set aside your life experiences when you are in a position to judge the way your refugee family behaves. Here are some true stories from our experience…

A generous person donated six brand new winter jackets, one for each member of the family, along with hats and mittens. We took the time to ensure that all the sizes where right for every person. Shortly thereafter the oldest daughter started telling people on our resettlement team that "we need coats." Didn't they like the ones we already provided? Didn't they appreciate all the work we went through to get them? Don't they realize how much they cost and the value of the donation that was made? How ungrateful! Then an inexpensive gift made all the difference. One day, after hearing the complaint, "we need coats," for the umpteenth time my wife picked up their picture dictionary and said, "Show me." The teenage girl pointed to a picture of a sweater. They had no sweaters and were simply too cold in school. Everyone assumed that since we could understand the sentence as it was spoken, that it was the right sentence. One word led to misunderstanding, judgment, and hurt feelings. How easy it was to fix the problem once true understanding was known.

One time we were told that the father in one of our refugee families was at the hospital. We had someone go to the hospital to learn what had happened and see if any help was needed. There was no sign of the man there or having been there. Eventually we learned that he had gone to a medical clinic for an immunization. Again, this was a simple misunderstanding because of the incorrect use of a common word.

A donor gave a generous gift of department store gift cards valued at $100/person in the family. That was $600 in this case. This donation was given within 30 days of the family's arrival so they did not yet comprehend normal life in our country. We explained that it might be good to buy some cold weather clothing since they had come from a much warmer country. Our very useful and practical advice was ignored even after we had an interpreter explain our point of view. Instead, they bought a camcorder and extra battery. We felt they blew their money on something frivolous. Indeed, once they got the camcorder home they didn't know how to use it or even how to read the instructions. They thought they could record video of their new life here and send tapes back home to their relatives, who would *also not have the technology to watch it. Yet, to them the value was more than the money. A camcorder was a tangible product that they perceived as something they could sell or barter later if they ever needed something else.*

It is easy for us to get frustrated when exhibited behaviors don't fit our model of expectations. Try to set aside your judgments and look at the people, where they have been, and what the situation might mean from their perspective. The more you realize that the lives of the refugees may have been completely different from your own, the more likely you are to move from one unusual situation to another without thinking poorly of the family you are trying to assist. Of course, you need to tell and teach, but you have to let them learn in their own time as they gain new experiences.

For an interesting judgment exercise, refer to the free materials at www.10milliontol.com/extras. Here you will find some examples of situational judgments. Work with your committee to become comfortable expecting the unexpected.

Choosing Interpreters

Sometimes you get lucky and find an interpreter who can help you communicate with your new refugee family. If there is a population in your area that speaks the language of your refugee family, it is likely that someone would be interested in helping out. Keep in mind that many refugees know more than one language. Even if you're not able to find an interpreter in their primary language, maybe someone speaks their second or third language.

Ideally, a qualified interpreter is competent both linguistically and culturally. You can check with your caseworker to see if there are any local options that are available and affordable. If such an interpreter is available, but costly, use them only for critical conversations, and find other options for day-to-day topics.

For medical issues, health departments and hospitals can access the AT&T translator hotline. Title VI of the Civil Rights Act requires them to provide meaningful access to services in the language of the client. There should be no charge for the cost of these interpreting services in this situation. With the objectivity and language competence of those on the hotline, this is the proper solution for medical communication.

In some cases, we have had to use a child as an interpreter. This is not an ideal situation, as complex ideas can get lost in the process. Or, they might get put into situations they cannot comprehend or come into information that is just too much for their young minds. Only rely on children as a last resort. Medical exams are not suitable for child interpreters.

For most communication, it's generally better to find someone else in the community that can help. The caution here is that they might not be as objective as you'd like. They may be opinionated or judgmental. They may be traumatized by what the refugee might say. The interpreter may not understand the need for confidentiality and may gossip to other community members. And, even though they speak the same language, they might be from an ethnicity that has been known to perpetrate violence toward the newcomer's ethnicity. How well will they interpret if any of these are true?

Once you have an interpreter, make sure they understand the importance of confidentiality. Also, ensure that your refugee family is comfortable with the interpreter you've chosen. This is important if you want them to readily share their thoughts and feelings.

Talking Through Interpreters

Before the conversation begins, spend a couple minutes with the interpreter to help them understand the context of the conversation that is to follow. Besides setting the proper foundation for discussion, it allows the interpreter to decide whether they can handle the topic and get help if they cannot do it alone.

When you are communicating with your refugee family using an interpreter there are some guidelines you should follow. First, always remember that you're really talking to the refugee, not the interpreter.

Therefore, you should be looking at the person you're talking to and speaking directly to them, not the interpreter.

Try to keep your sentences short. Also, ask the person to whom you're talking to communicate in short simple sentences. This is good etiquette as it helps the interpreter and helps keep the conversation moving. Keep in mind that it can be difficult for interpreters to handle a lot of information at a time. Consider talking to someone for a couple minutes and then ask him or her to repeat what you've said back to you. Odds are they will miss something. Now, if you force that same person to repeat what you've said, but in a different language, you have created a complicated scenario. Keep it all in short bursts, and the job is much easier.

Sometimes during the course of conversation, someone will speak for a long time and then the interpreter may just say a few words. It could be that the interpreter is having difficulty, or it might mean they got on a side tangent of conversation. Possibly the interpreter felt he needed more information to give an accurate interpretation. It may be good for the interpreter to have additional information, but not to your exclusion. You should have access to that information as well. Likewise when you are talking, make sure the interpreter passes along all your commentary. Politely ask that everything, regardless of who is speaking, be interpreted. If you still feel you're missing something, you might even ask, "What else was said?"

If, during the conversation, you uncover information that the refugee's caseworker should know, be sure you pass along the information. If the caseworker provided the interpreter, he or she may take back the information, but do not assume that they will. Either discuss with the interpreter who will mention the situation, or else just go ahead and bring it up on your own. The caseworker won't be upset with too much information.

Communicating Without Interpreters

Sometimes you will not have the luxury of an interpreter. What then? As adults, we tend to rely on verbal communication and sometimes feel stuck if we cannot work at our normal conversational level.

Our first refugee family lived in our house for a week before they were able to move into their apartment. We did not speak their language. They spoke little English, practically none at that point in time. Our children were 4 and 7 years old. The refugee children were 11, 11, and 16. One evening all of the kids were outside throwing a Frisbee having fun. The adults joined in. No spoken word was necessary to have fun. That doesn't mean we were silent. We all spoke our own language, and even believed we understood each other at times. Words were important, but common language was not.

Our son, the 7 year old, had a video game system that he showed to the 11-year-old boy. They spent hours playing games together, getting to know each other, just having fun. Later, we were talking to our son about how much he enjoyed playing with this older boy. We brought up the point that the refugee boy didn't speak English and what our son thought about that. Our son had not noticed. He said with surprise, "He doesn't speak English? But I always understand him." You see, it just didn't matter. They got along fine. Each understood the meaning through the context, not by the words.

A final example. With each family that has stayed at our house, or when we first invited the family to our house for dinner for those who did not stay with us, I would always get out some maps. First, a map of the world. I would point to the United States saying, "This is the United States. We live here." I would point to our approximate area. Then I would pull out a state map. "This is our state, Wisconsin. We live here." I would point to our city. Then I would go back to the world map. I would name their country, point to it, and ask where they live. Regardless of language spoken, they always understood. Sometimes I would pull out an encyclopedia or atlas to get a better map of their country so they could point to their hometown. Sometimes they would express where they lived their normal life and then show where they lived as refugees before coming to the U.S. We always enjoy this conversation.

So, how do you speak without an interpreter? Start using short sentences, speak slowly, and try to use simple, basic words. If you're lucky, they will have had some exposure to English somewhere in the past. They might know a few words. Combine that with the context of the conversation and you might do OK. Pause frequently, trying to make sure they understand. If you don't think they understood, try again. See if you can use even simpler language, adding gestures and pantomime. You can even attempt to draw pictures. Avoid big words, professional buzzwords, colloquialisms, and slang. They will not understand these things.

Another way to communicate is through pantomime and imitation of animals. For example, while grocery shopping, sometimes the cuts of meat the refugees see in our butcher shops are not easily recognized. My wife has been seen clucking like a chicken and flapping her arms like wings to describe a skinless, boneless chicken breast. Sure, she got strange looks from the locals, but everyone understood her point. What's the difference between a cut of pork and a hunk of beef? Oink like a pig or moo like a cow. Mooing in the grocery store has never failed to get some good laughs, but they also understand. If this behavior is too far out of your comfort zone, I would suggest shopping with a picture dictionary so you can point to a picture of the animal. This isn't as amusing, but it's still quite effective.

If you are trying to communicate instructions, consider writing them down, and then explain. Leave them with the written instructions. They might be able to find someone who can translate for them later. This will reinforce your verbal explanation.

Keep in mind that most people receive politeness quite well. "Please" and "thank you" can go a long way to keeping good feelings during tougher conversations. Be respectful, empathize, always show appreciation for their situation, and be ready to offer encouragement at any time.

One last point, remember the value of a smile. If you are able to smile, most people will understand that things must be OK. They will relax and be open to the conversation. If things start to get tense, it's OK to rely on some humor. While styles and preferences of humor differ around the world and even between individuals in the same culture, it does promote laughter and reduces tension. Even if you only succeed in making yourself laugh (my wife accuses me of this all the time), at least you are more in a position to handle whatever is coming your way. Smile big.

To help you consider communication without language, refer to the communication exercise in the bonus materials at www.10milliontol. com/extras. Try this with your resettlement team before your refugee family arrives.

CHAPTER 8

OTHER LESSONS

I was 15 years old, fleeing my homeland to a refugee camp with a group of about 30 people. We were all carrying food and our personal belongings. The enemy was aggressively pursuing us. As we took some rest we had to hide among trees to stay safe. When I opened my eyes I saw one of the gunmen with his weapon pointed directly at me. We looked at each other. I knew he would have to shoot me and the others. That was his job. His life would depend on it.

Just then he raised his gun and shot into the tree top. Thankfully, this gave me and our group an opportunity to escape. The other gunmen began shooting as well. I dropped everything and ran; abandoning the bag I was carrying which included the only picture I owned, one of my mother. Everyone else ran too, splitting up for survival. One woman, the mother of a young boy, was shot. No one could go back to help without also being shot. We assume she was killed. That day the rest of us lived.

Now I wonder, did the gunman that first saw me come to a realization that he couldn't shoot me point blank? Or was he just looking for the challenge of shooting moving targets? Or was he cruelly exerting his power by scaring us all first with a shot in the air? Or did he hate his job, truly not wanting to kill anyone but yet maintain his tough image with his colleagues? I will never know, but I am grateful to be alive.

Handling Money

As mentioned in the Finance Team section, your refugee family's understanding and handling of money is a key element in their development as an independent, self-sufficient, functional family in the U.S. economy. Their early experiences can help them to develop a credit history that they will need for years to come.

For those of us who have lived in the U.S. for our entire life, our credit history has developed over time by accident or via deliberate steps. It will be no different for your refugee family. Either you will help them move forward in an intentional, deliberate manner or their history will be defined by the accidents that happen along the way.

Unlike most Americans, refugees have no debt when they arrive. Well, that's not quite true. They have a little debt, but none of it has come due yet. We'll get to this in a few moments. For now, let's consider that they have no debt.

When it's time to work out their budget, which I would recommend you do within their first week, you have it easy. You can look at expenses and project income. They have no baggage on their lives. They are, quite literally, "starting over."

So, what are the expenses: rent, food, electricity, gas, water, telephone service, and miscellaneous things like personal care items, cleaning supplies, clothing, and some money for transportation. For someone on low income, spending on the miscellaneous things can, and should, be quite low. Put together an expense budget, one item at a time, with a number for all of the adults in the family to see. Estimate the expenses on a monthly basis. For some refugees this number will be higher than their best annual salary and they will be shocked.

Show the family's initial income. Perhaps they are eligible for food stamps (or an equivalent program) worth about $100 per month per person. Perhaps they will receive a welfare (or similar public assistance) check monthly. Instead, they might receive some grant money through the sponsoring refugee agency. Whatever their source of non-working income, what is the total? Add this to the value of their food stamps. What's the total income for the month? How does this compare to the expenses?

Most of the time you will find that the expenses exceed the "free" money. This is the object lesson in demonstrating the importance of finding a job as soon as possible. They will not be able to survive their expenses without a job. For some refugees this will be very scary. You can see it non-verbally on their face. They are wondering if coming to America is all they thought it would be. Suddenly they become aware that the roads are not paved with gold, and they will not enjoy handouts the rest of their lives. For others the thought of going to work and earning a living is the most exciting aspect of stepping onto our shores. They have been denied the ability to be productive and to feel good about it. Now they have an opportunity, and you have just given them a strong motivation to get started.

Regardless of their reaction to your news, you must reassure them that your resettlement committee is here to help them. You will help them pay for rent (likely the most costly expense) at least in part for several months. You are here to help them find a job so that they can earn the money they need.

Now, assume that you can find a single job at $7.25 per hour, working 40 hours per week. That's approximately $1,250 per month. Assume the "free" money they were looking at before goes away. How does $1,250 compare to the expenses? Does it still fall short? If so, this demonstrates the need for the spouse to go to work. (Note that it is expected that all adults will find employment.) If there is no spouse, is there an older child that can find a part-time minimum wage job? If your refugee family consists of a single parent with no working-age children, and the monthly expenses cannot be met, then you have a problem. However, in this case it is likely that public assistance benefits may not go away completely. Check to see what level of financial and food support may remain and add that to the $1,250. If the numbers still don't work consider $8/hour. That's about $1,385 per month.

Point out that the potential income of the spouse and/or working child will generate extra income beyond the requirements. This is the money that they can use to improve their situation. They can use that extra money to buy the fun things they want, or eventually move to a nicer apartment, or they can save it to purchase a car, or even their own house someday.

Back to the issue of refugee debt. They actually do arrive in our country with an obligation to repay the airfare that brought them here. Before they depart for the U.S., they agree to repay transportation expenses that they received from the U.S. Department of State via the IOM. The U.S. government pays their one-way travel to our country with an interest-free loan. The agreement is that the refugee family will earn money to pay back Uncle Sam for the courtesy tickets. The money paid back goes into the same fund and can help bring another family. (If the family fails to pay their loan, future resettlement can be limited until new funding becomes available.)

Within three or four months of arrival, your refugee family should receive a reminder of their travel loan along with information about how to make their first payment. Generally, that payment is due by the end of their sixth month. If employment has not yet been obtained, or other financial circumstances make this loan exceptionally difficult at that time, it is possible to get an extension. It is also possible to reduce the monthly payments and lengthen the term. Work with your sponsoring agency to make any needed adjustments.

Once payments begin, the family will typically have three years to pay off their obligation, though sometimes less if the amount is small. Some families like to pay off their loan early, and this gives them a good feeling of accomplishment.

As a co-sponsor, you might also receive the repayment information. It is for your understanding, not your obligation. This is payment for a benefit previously received by the refugee family. They have agreed to pay it and you should allow them to do so. If neither you nor they have received repayment information within four months of arrival, call the sponsoring agency caseworker to check on the status.

Sometimes people are offended that the government would make this a requirement of the refugees. Yet, I believe there are several good reasons to do this. First, for those in the community that are opposed to helping refugees (yes, there are some) one of their arguments is that helping refugees costs the taxpayers money. If the refugees must pay back their airfare, then that part is not a taxpayer expense. Second, they will pay back the airfare in small monthly installments over several years. The regular paying back of this loan helps establish a credit history. For this reason it is best to allow the refugee family to make this payment themselves, on time, month after month.

We've heard donors who have offered to pay back the airfare. We explain the importance of the family's learning to pay debts in a timely manner and the establishment of a credit history. Then we politely refuse this offer. However, it is likely that the donor's money could be used elsewhere. How would they like to contribute toward a month's rent instead?

Even if donors wish to help with rent, we recommend only fully covering the first month or two. After this, we would like to have the refugee family contributing. Even if they are living on public assistance only, it might help them feel better if they are helping to pay their way. In addition, it starts to develop their habit of writing checks and paying on time. Maybe they only pay $50 or $100 at first. Once they get a job, increase their payment over a couple months so that the shock of full payment doesn't come on too suddenly.

For one of our families we had a donor offer to pay three months' rent. We used their money to pay the first month in full. Then we applied the rest to the next four months, paying less each month. The refugee family paid more each month. For the sixth month, our rent payment was just $100 with the family paying the majority. A week prior to that, the father in the family started his first permanent job. Our rent payments stopped and they were already transitioned to making payments on their own. They had the necessary income and the habit to do it.

Finding a Job

Refugees are rarely successful in getting jobs by the conventional method of seeing a job opening and submitting an application. Imagine what their application looks like to an employer. They have no job history in the US. They may not be able to substantiate any educational details. Any information of substance is barely pronounceable, including the name of the applicant. What would motivate an employer to pick up the phone and even make a follow-up call? There are several steps you can take to give the refugees a fighting chance for a job.

Fill out the job application, or have the refugee fill out the application. Include a cover letter explaining the refugee's situation and include a local, English speaking person as a contact for the prospective employer. The local contact, in most cases, should be someone on the employment team. The exception is if someone else personally knows the employer. In that case, use the relationship. Include a personal reference statement in the cover letter as well. Stress the applicant's attendance record in an ESL program, strong work ethic, fast learner, intense desire to work, whatever is appropriate and truthful.

Be present with the applicant when dropping off the application and at the interview. The most effective way to help refugees get a job is to go to bat for them with the employer, either on the phone or in person. Try to talk directly to the people that make the hiring decisions. If you know that individual personally, they will trust your judgment. If there is no personal connection, you might need to "sell" the idea to the hiring manager. Of course, any time you can use the "it's who you know" method, you stand a better chance of helping the refugee find a job in a hurry.

Refusing a Job

We had been trying to get a job for the father in one refugee family for over a year. It was difficult due to some physical limitations. We had found several jobs that he would qualify for and could handle physically.

But, he turned down the jobs for various reasons. "That's a woman's job." "The hours are bad." "It doesn't pay enough." The idea that a job didn't pay enough was too much for me to take. We had already shown the math that the job <u>did</u> pay enough. It was just that he knew someone else who was earning more money and he wanted to be paid similarly, yet he was not able to perform a comparable job due to his physical handicap.

One day I had to point out that you can't just jump into your ideal pay scale. Sometimes you have to start with something to gain experience and work history. Then you can move up. After the next turned down offer we would no longer help him find a job. He would be on his own. Ironically, after we gave up trying to help, he received a call back from a temp agency within a week. Shortly thereafter he had accepted a job. He was more independent than we gave him credit to be.

What if the refugee family members are offered a job and refuse to take it? This is not that uncommon a situation. For whatever reason they may believe that a particular job is not suitable. Depending on your employment assistance programs, refusing a job might result in loss of assistance benefits. Before arriving in the U.S. your family also had been told that they must accept a full time job if they are offered one. While they are adults, they ultimately can decide what to do. It is your job to explain the consequences of a poor decision. Will they lose benefits? How will they pay for rent? How will they find a different job on their own? Will you continue to support their efforts, or will their rejection of a job also mean rejection of your help? Saying no to the opportunity to work is not a responsible decision. Help them understand that they can always change to a new job when a better one comes along. But for now, it is important that they accept any job to start earning money and move toward self-sufficiency.

Telephone Usage

Many refugees will want to call home. Immediately upon their arrival, it is a good idea to let them do this. Help them make a brief call from your house, your cell phone, or a public phone. They, and any friends or family left behind, will appreciate this opportunity. Let them do this at your committee's expense.

After this, you need to make it clear that international long distance is expensive and they are responsible for their own telephone bills. For now, the least expensive method to make international calls is to purchase a prepaid international calling card. A $5 card might allow as much as 60-90 minutes or more even to some out-of-the-way countries. We've had good luck buying these cards at local gas stations owned or operated by immigrants.

A prepaid calling card can be used at any phone by placing a call to a toll free number. When the call is answered, you enter the calling card number followed by the destination phone number. Read the instructions on the card for complete details. Also, note that calls to international sites will start with the international code of 011, followed by a country code, a city or area code, and then the local phone number. It might take some experimenting to get the number correct.

Eventually your refugee family will get a phone of their own. Suddenly they have the convenience of dialing direct without needing a calling card. Unless they subscribe to a discounted international calling program, direct dialing is a very costly mistake. While they might be able to talk for an hour on a $5 calling card, it is not unheard of to reach $100 or more in an hour of direct-dialed conversation. Over the course of a month, they could easily end up with a phone bill nearing $500.

Another potential problem is that of accepting collect calls. Collect calls generally cost even more than direct-dialed calls. It is not uncommon for overseas relatives to call collect. They feel that their family members who have made it to America are in a better place and can afford the service. Neither party is usually aware of the steep cost. The family that has made it to the U.S. might even feel guilty about living here while they still have loved ones left behind. This may make it difficult for them to refuse a collect call.

That first phone bill can be an eye-opening experience and a painful lesson. If, despite your warnings, your family runs up a large phone bill, you can offer to help them out. No, you're not going to pay their bill! You can call the phone company to explain the situation and see if there are any calling plans that would have made these calls much more economical. Sometimes the phone company may issue a partial credit if you subscribe to an appropriate calling plan. Sometimes they may even retroactively recalculate the bill at the plan rate. Regardless of the outcome, the phone bill is a consequence of the refugee family's actions. They must live with this consequence and pay this bill. If they choose to pay it over time, the phone company might block service until it is paid in full. Odds are good this problem won't happen again.

Let Them Pay Their Own Bills

Paying bills is an integral part of our life. Self-sufficiency is not attained until the family is able to pay their own bills without your assistance. You should have established a checking account as soon as possible. By the time the first bill arrives, they will have temporary checks or maybe their personalized checks will have arrived. Either way, make them part of the bill paying experience.

Writing a check may be something completely new to your family. Heck, writing may even be something completely new for them. Therefore, for the first bill, you should write it out, explaining each component of the check. Show whom you're writing it to and that it matches the name on the bill. Show the amount and that it matches the number on the bill. Show that it is necessary to write the amount both as a number and in longhand. And, finally, have them sign the check. They can sign the check with their original signature in their own script or alphabet as long as it matches what they have on file at the bank. Sometimes it helps to write the English version of their name under their signature so that the recipient can read it as matching the name on the check. Put the bill with the check in an envelope and apply appropriate postage. If they have a mailbox, show them how to send the mail. If you have to take it to a drop-box or the post office, you'll eventually have to show them how to do this on their own. As a convenience, you may wish to mail these first pieces yourself, along with your own mail.

For the next bills that come up, see if someone in your refugee family can write. Show him or her how to fill out the checks. Point out the significant items and where they must be written. You might even want to write out each component on a separate piece of paper as a guide. The family can keep that guide for future reference. For very important payments, like monthly apartment rent, it can be helpful to provide a complete check template that they can keep with their checkbook and copy each month. If no one in the family can write, you can still work through this exercise; you'll just have to wait a bit longer before turning over the responsibility.

Fire Prevention

Unless there is an overhead sprinkler system in the selected housing, you must ensure there is a working smoke detector present. Whether the law requires it in your area is irrelevant. This is a vital consideration. Test to verify that the smoke detector works, and confirm that the family understands it. If either of these conditions is not true, do not allow the family to move into the new apartment.

Likewise, every home should have a fire extinguisher. Keep it in a convenient area where everyone can find it. Take some time to make sure that all the family members know when and how to use it.

Appliances

Your refugee family may not be familiar with our standard set of household appliances.

Demonstrate how to use the stove, oven, and microwave oven. An oven seems obvious, but people from some cultures have never used one, and might not even know what one is. We've seen families use an oven as an extra storage area for canned goods. Instead of just pointing out where the oven is, consider actually demonstrating it. Perhaps you set aside a few hours to provide in depth training on a number of appliances. With the oven, you could bake cookies or a cake with the family. When you're done everyone understands the usage, and they have a nice treat to share.

Likewise, many refugees are completely unfamiliar with a microwave oven. You may have to demonstrate, and communicate what can and what cannot go into a microwave oven. Again, it is not a storage area.

Talk about the refrigerator too. While we consider a refrigerator standard, and a necessity, many people have never had one. They learn to gather their food daily instead of keeping it cold and preserved for days at a time. You may have to explain which foods need refrigeration and which do not. Explain that some foods won't go into the refrigerator until after they are opened or cooked, while others should be placed in the refrigerator right away. Make sure they have appropriate storage containers as well as plastic wrap and aluminum foil to keep things freshest. After several weeks, we discovered one of our families was storing their cooked leftovers in a cupboard instead of the refrigerator. That might prevent the flies from landing on it, but it doesn't keep it good to eat. On the other side of the coin, you might also find them storing boxed or canned goods in the refrigerator or freezer. Clearly, that is not necessary. In light of these situations, you should consider checking their food storage habits more than once.

The washing machine and dryer may be foreign concepts as well. We've had several families who were happy washing their clothes in a sink or bathtub and hang dry. While this may be OK at first, avoiding appliance-learning overload, they may eventually want to know the easier way to do laundry. Some families may already be used to washers and dryers. In that case, they will want to have that convenience right away. If washers and dryers are available in their apartment building, or you gave them their own, show them proper usage including what soap to use in the washer. If they don't have these appliances available, start them off with a roll of quarters, and show them how to get to the laundromat.

Junk Mail

When we bring in our own mail for the day we find things we're happy to receive, we find bills to pay, and we find a lot of "junk mail." Having grown up in the U.S., we can quickly sort our mail, throwing away or recycling the junk, without a second thought. Imagine you just arrived in a strange land and you get mail. You can't even read it. How do you know what is important and what is not? You don't. You have to learn.

At first, someone on your resettlement team should take a look at all mail that comes in. Have your family put it all in a safe place. Every time someone visits, he or she can look at the mail. Point out all of the "real" mail; including bills and communication from social services. Save the bills to help them pay at the appropriate time. Read any communication from social services. These may simply be reports or status updates. On the other hand, they may require action. Save any items that require action for the appropriate committee member(s). Point out the "junk" mail and indicate that they do not need it. Say, "this is garbage" and throw it away. They will understand.

Over time, allow the family to decide, while you are there, what they believe is junk. Confirm whether they are correct or not. Once they are able to correctly identify the junk, they should be allowed to do this, just saving the important things for your review. Eventually they will recognize the bills and pay them, file the things they need to keep, throw away the junk, and just ask you questions at those times when they are unsure.

Telemarketers

Comparable to junk mail, your refugee family may not understand the concept of telephone solicitations. And, even if the concept is understood, the language probably won't be. Unknowingly they could agree to purchase something because of saying yes when they should have said no. The best action they can take, when they don't know the caller, is to simply explain they don't speak English well, and then hang up. If the phone rings again, they can let the caller go to their answering machine so that someone else can determine the nature of the call. If your state has a "no call" list, I would recommend putting your refugee family's phone number on that list to minimize potential annoyances.

Some refugees get worried or scared when they pick up a ringing telephone and there is no one on the other end. Sometimes the delay caused by telemarketing computer dialing systems is enough to bring disturbing images to their minds. They perceive these calls to represent some kind of hidden danger; perhaps a violent enemy stalker, a harassing government, or even a hostile neighbor who wants to get them to leave their apartment. Whatever the source of such calls, just explain that if they are ever uncomfortable with an incoming call, they should just hang up.

Income Taxes

When the adults in the refugee family get jobs, they will start to encounter federal, and perhaps state, income taxes. There are two approaches to handling taxes that make sense. You will have to decide which scenario makes the most sense for your family's situation.

Option 1. Select an estimate of the proper number of deductions for that family that will result in their getting a small refund when they file their tax return. You want them to get money back because odds are they won't have money left to pay a bill that they won't understand. Yet, they will be excited at the extra money that comes their way once each year. It works as kind of a forced savings plan. You won't want to force too great of taxes though and cripple their take home income. So plan a good balance.

Option 2. Some families will be sufficiently large and have low-end employment such that they would qualify for earned income credit (EIC). These credits can be applied all year long to increase the take home pay of the recipient. As long as this situation does not produce a tax bill, go for it. The EIC can make each check a little more supportive of the family.

Some refugees will have a clear understanding of taxes. Others will have no concept at all. To explain taxes you can simply say that a portion of each paycheck has to go to the government. You are there to help them. Work directly with their employer to choose exemptions or fill out their paperwork. You should decide what makes the most sense rather than trying to have the family understand exactly what you are trying to accomplish.

The first year, maybe the next few too if you feel inclined, you should offer to help with filing their income tax return. If someone on your resettlement team has any connections with an accountant or interested party willing to help for no charge, pursue that angle. Otherwise if someone on your team would like to take it on him or herself that would also be OK. Usually the tax form can be the simplest form since there are no excessive deductions or unusual circumstances for a newly arrived refugee family. They simply have income earned and taxes withheld. EIC might be an additional consideration.

CHAPTER 9

REFUGEE REACTIONS AND RESPONSES

I was at my job, working in a factory, doing what I could to help support my family through some tough times. Suddenly the rebels came in and started questioning, "who here is Muslim?" All who raised their hands were shot and killed. This was crazy because we used to have a society that was well integrated and had religious tolerance.

Nearly all refugees will go through five stages in their adaptation to a new life. It is important that you understand and recognize these stages. These are normal, though not always easy to deal with.

Stage 1 is the **survival** stage. This is like the honeymoon stage of a marriage. They have just escaped from their old life, and for the first time in a long time, things are going well. Refugees have learned to adapt and this is just another adaptation. They, and you, can focus on their basic needs. They will generally comply with any requests you make or any schedules you dictate. They will bond to your helping and are most often willing to please you. They are grateful, though they often don't know how to express their gratitude especially if language is a difficulty. During this stage they are very dependent on you and your resettlement team.

Stage 2 is the **reality** stage. Now that survival is certain, they have a chance to reflect on all that has happened to this point. It is now that a whole array of emotions starts to kick in. They may feel frustrated by slow progress and dealing with "the system." They may have sadness or guilt over their lives or family and friends that they left behind. They may be angry because life doesn't seem as easy as they had hoped, or they feel they may never really understand our world.

This stage is also the most difficult for you. Since you have developed some bonds with the refugee family, your team is likely to be at the forefront receiving all their emotion. They need to vent and you're in just the right place with the right amount of trust and closeness. When they need a shoulder to cry on, you can provide it. When they express guilt, lend your understanding. Their anger and frustrations are the most difficult to deal with. You don't want to minimize them or make it appear that their concerns are unimportant. You must be careful to avoid internalizing their anger or thinking that you've done something wrong. If you make that mistake you risk spoiling your resettlement experience. You've got to push through, listen to their concerns, make adjustments or provide help when necessary, and let go of the rest. Do not take it personally.

Stage 3 is the **bottoming out** stage. This stage sounds worse than stage 2. For the refugees it is, for you it is not. With any luck, this stage is very short or even absorbed into stage 2. In that case, you're already dealing with it and helping their recovery as part of your actions in stage 2.

Some signs of reaching stage 3 include less interest in carrying out normal tasks, occasional tardiness to work or school, or perhaps not being ready on time for various appointments. Normally you can just stress the importance of punctuality and maintaining their life as you've taught them. They will get through it without much problem.

On the other hand, if this stage is pronounced, you need to seek professional help for the family or some of the family members. You will observe a number of warning signs if stage 3 is becoming serious. These may include continuing depression or a desire to withdraw from you, their work, school, or other activities. They may skip appointments altogether without notifying anyone. They may develop aches and pains that appear to have no physical cause. They may fail to follow through on the easiest of ordinary tasks. They may demonstrate high levels of anxiety or agitation and may be suffering from loss of sleep or nightmares. If these signs appear please consult your resettlement agency's case worker. These signs may indicate the need for assessment and treatment by a mental health professional.

Stage 4 is the **acceptance** stage. Things start to get good again in this stage. The refugees are coming to accept their new home and environment. They are beginning to create friendships outside of your resettlement committee. They start to feel as though they belong. When they compare the past with the present, their outlook starts to sound more positive. They realize that life isn't the same as it was, but that they are going to be OK, that their current short-term struggles are not part of their previous struggles.

In this stage they start to become more goal oriented, not just living day-to-day. They are generally reliable in their jobs and at school. They might start expressing desires to improve their situation further through additional vocational training or greater interest in learning English. They may start making changes to their living space, adapting it to reflect their own preferences. It is fun to visit their apartment once they've started changing the decorations and furniture to meet their tastes. Some families may even express interest in moving to a new location of their choice that feels more comfortable for them.

Emotionally they become more stable. The highs may not be as high as you saw in stages 1 and 2, but the lows are not nearly as low as in stages 2 and 3. They show more emotional integrity and higher levels of self-confidence. Children will show fewer behavioral problems and start performing better in school as well, making new friends, and starting to enjoy classes and even sports.

For you stage 4 becomes fun again. You start to see that you have made a lasting impression on their lives. The rewards of seeing your efforts pay off in the development of a self-sufficient refugee family might cause your own emotional release. You feel the accomplishment of helping them not only settle in this country, but also of having helped them get through stage 2 and past stage 3. When you get into stage 4 to stay, or move into stage 5, pat yourself on the back and consider a party to celebrate!

Stage 5 is the **resolution** stage. The refugee family really starts their new life here. They have passed through the difficult stages and have accepted their situation. In general, they don't need you anymore. The family becomes goal and future oriented. They start seeing the possibilities for their lives. They want to be independent, and they will assert that desire. They may still need assistance with certain resources including help when it becomes possible for them to apply for Green Cards, but overall, they will let go of you just as you have been letting go of them.

Signs of Refugee Trauma

As I stated above, stage 2 is the most difficult for you to deal with and stage 3 is the toughest for the refugees. We need to dig a little deeper here so that you can better recognize some of the signs present in these stages as well as have an understanding about how you should respond.

In stage 2 or 3, you may see some signs of the trauma experienced by your refugee family. Those signs may be brief in stage 2 or very pronounced in stage 3, especially if any of the family members are manifesting Post-traumatic Stress Disorder. Here are some of the symptoms that may begin to appear:

- Memory and concentration problems. They just don't seem as "with it" as they did previously. Where they might have been getting to work and school on time, now they might be late. Setting and sticking to priorities becomes more difficult.
- Fatigue. They may simply be more worn out or may be suffering from sleep problems. In some cases, they may be intentionally staying awake at night fearing for the safety of their family. In other cases, it just might be that the accumulated sleep deficit of the past weeks or months is catching up to them.

- Distrust. While they may have trusted you implicitly in the beginning, they now begin to question your motives. They may worry about losing their job, being forced to move again, or even being sent to another country.
- Survivor's guilt. Since they are now safe, they may fear for family left behind, or feel guilt for being alive when others they know may have been killed, tortured, or imprisoned.
- Hyper-arousal. They may demonstrate extreme reactions to loud voices or other noises. They may startle easy or get into arguments over minor issues.
- Grief or powerlessness. You may see sadness like never before. They may not feel in control; the world has changed too much; they can't do what they used to do. Where they previously appeared as if they could handle anything, now they're down and uncertain of the future.
- Flashbacks. Old memories come back, unwanted. They may feel and even react as if they're reliving a previous traumatic state.
- Dissociation. They begin to pull away from their own family and others. You may have difficulty communicating with them. This can be especially pronounced in teenagers.

Responding to Stages 2 and 3

Your refugees are not enjoying this time. Odds are neither are you. So what can you do to make the best of this time for your team, while offering the best level of support for your refugee family? Here are some suggestions to help you move the refugees into stage 4 and beyond.

- Provide clear expectations and instructions, regardless how simple and understandable you think it is.
- Keep their activities calendar up to date. This is a time where you should try to keep surprises to a minimum. If they can see it coming on the calendar they have a chance to prepare.

- Get them into a routine or on a specific schedule as quickly as you can. Predictable routines help develop habits. If they can get into a habit of doing something well, your efforts are easier.
- Don't run away from their frustrations. Acknowledge the frustrations even if you don't understand them.
- Give positive reinforcement for even the smallest thing that goes right. If you can help them feel good about something they did, you give them more confidence for the future.
- Strive for problem solving, not blame. Take ownership of the situation. If there's a school or employment matter assure those in charge that you'll help correct the situation.
- Help to make the home environment "normal." It should become part of their comfort zone. To get through the bottoming out of stage 3 they have to start feeling they have a place to go that is their own.
- Related to the last point, make sure they are absolutely safe in their environment. They don't need other things to worry about.
- If they need to talk about their trauma, let them. Just be there for them and listen. Hugs can go a long way too, though be careful of cultural contact issues.
- Be sensitive to any needed mourning. There is truly a sense of loss (country, family, friends, abilities, pride, etc.) that must be overcome.
- Try to get them more connected to their new community or the community of other natives from their country, whether refugees or other immigrants.
- If the situation warrants, seek professional advice. Sometimes mental health programs are available to work through the complicated cases. If in doubt, talk to their caseworker at the resettlement agency. They may offer advice or even direct the care.

The good news is that you and the family will get through these times, though not everyone in the family will necessarily be on the same time line. Stage 4 is on its way.

Finally, if you've stuck with the family all the way to stage 5, you've made a new friend. Now your relationship will be one of mutual friendship, based on the elements that make up any friendship, rather than the parent-child-dependency relationship in stage 1 or the caregiver-recipient relationship of stages 2 and 3. Congratulate yourself and your entire team for a job well done!

CHAPTER 10

FRIENDSHIP

I left home when I was 17 years old. I was on the run, left my country, and became a refugee. Now, 20 years later, it is still too dangerous for me to return home to visit my elderly parents. Recently, I was able to arrange for them to travel 150 miles from their home and get a one-day pass into the neighboring country. Here we could meet briefly, talk, exchange news, and then go our own ways once again. One day I hope the oppressive government is overthrown and people obtain broader freedoms again.

Our role in resettling refugees is not to carry them through a new life and make all their troubles go away. Rather, it is our responsibility to walk with them, guiding them and teaching them, so that they can develop into their new life. When the time is right, we can let them go. Or, they can let us go. When we all have the freedom to say goodbye, we might just find out that we made a new friend.

Becoming friends is a process. Just like meeting someone new in your neighborhood, your relationship develops over time until you reach a certain level and consider yourselves friends. Bridging the gap of culture and circumstances puts up some hurdles, but you can overcome these if you'll make some little efforts. The tips that follow will make the transition to your community easier for your refugee family. It will also propel your relationship forward.

Start out by learning a few words in their language. They are going to be making great strides to learn English. A little effort on your part to learn to say hello, thank you, and goodbye in their language can be a great comfort. You may be able to have them teach you these words or you can learn the words using other resources.

Try to understand something about their home country. Having a little information about the geography, current political situation, or history will help you to have a basis upon which to add the family's stories and their personal experiences. Understanding a little bit about their situation in their refugee camp or other temporary home can help round out your knowledge. Keep in mind though, that whatever you learn, you cannot truly empathize with them. Don't try. You cannot feel the pain they have felt or pretend to understand their situation, or the horrors they may have faced, without direct experience.

When invited, be sure to try their foods. Not only will your acceptance of their food be a compliment to them, but also you might discover a great new flavor! Could you get this experience at a local restaurant? Or would you otherwise have to travel to their country as a tourist to get this taste experience? Here's your chance to try authentic cuisine from around the world.

Odds are at some point you will do something that they will consider culturally inappropriate. Avoid the attitude that they're here now so they have to learn our way. While that statement may be true, arrogance instead of cultural sensitivity will not advance a friendship. Seek a way to correct your error and learn their culture. This way you can advance them into our culture while using theirs as a stepping-stone. Don't forget the power of a smile and a little humility to fix things. You're learning along with them.

On the other side, they are also likely to do or say things that are not considered appropriate in our culture. Typically, we do not talk about our salaries or how much we paid for our house. However, they might not have these stigmas and may freely ask such questions in their efforts to learn about us. Since you are their mentor, answer if you wish. Whether you answer or not, it is good to point out the things that may offend other Americans. It's much better for them to get a lesson from you than to be judged poorly by a stranger.

Some refugees will share their personal stories with you very early in the relationship. Others will take some time. Still others may never be comfortable enough to share. Perhaps the memories are too painful. It is best to hear their stories at a time of their choosing, when they are comfortable. Therefore, I would not recommend asking for their stories unless, and until, you have really become close friends.

Difficult Topics

From time to time, there are topics of discussion that you must lead but which may not be comfortable for you or your refugee family. Sometimes we find the best way to deal with an issue is play the role of a parent offering "tough love." You know the right action that your refugee family should take, but they don't understand the reasons and may resist your advice. By standing firm and not bailing them out, they will learn a valuable lesson that helps them cope in the future.

Sometimes you will realize that tough love is not appropriate. There are cases where an "intervention" is necessary. Perhaps the intervention can solve the problem before it comes to tough love. Perhaps the lesson is simply not being learned on its own. Either way it requires that you step in, as a friend, to straighten out the perspective and help the family better fit into our society.

A clear example of the latter is the issue of body odor. In many cultures around the world, people do not take personal hygiene as seriously as here in the U.S. We have had this discussion, to one degree or another, with nearly every family that we have resettled. This is not a discussion for the first day, or even the first week. In some cases, the family may realize our obsessions and adapt on their own. But in time, if that change does not occur, this is an important topic. After all, a person with a strong body smell will not be well accepted in a job or in public. It is our job to help them fit in our society. If they don't notice this difference then we have to help them understand. This is an issue best performed through an interpreter so that the "why" can be explained. If no interpreter is available, you may have the conversation several times before the understanding gets through. Through the interpreter, explain that in our culture people don't want to smell other people. It is better they hear this from a friend than from a stranger on the bus, or from their employer as they are walked out the door. Worse yet, what if they can't get a job because of the smell and no one tells them why?

Regardless of the difficult topic, take some time to consider the message you want to communicate. Then you can find an appropriate time to have the conversation. Keep in mind that you are presenting the information as a friend and you are doing this out of love. You don't have to be embarrassed or shy about it. It's likely that whatever stigma our society places on the issue, that they do not have that same perspective. That's why the problem arises in the first place. So, be matter-of-fact in describing the problem, the solution, and why this is important. Most likely, you will see an improvement. If, after some time, the improvement is not enough, repeat the discussion.

Applying for a Green Card - Lawful Permanent Residence

The Green Card, whether colored green or not, is the term which applies to Lawful Permanent Residence (LPR) Status. Refugees, upon arrival in the U.S., already have most rights allowed to those with LPR status. The only exception is that they do not receive guaranteed reentry into the U.S. if they leave for some reason. After obtaining their Green Card, they are free to come and go as they please, as they are eligible for a U.S. Passport.

The process of getting to lawful permanent resident status is much too complicated for refugee families to do on their own. It's also too important a process to get wrong. There are cases where families have had minor oversights that caused them to be denied. Then they have to either appeal or resubmit, starting the whole process again. Even though your time with the family has significantly lessened by this time, it will help them greatly if you step back in to help with the LPR application process. (Note that your supporting resettlement agency may handle this task completely. If so, you still might want to be involved. At a minimum, remind the agency when the family has been here a year, just to make sure the ball isn't dropped.)

The family cannot obtain a Green Card until they have been in the U.S. for at least a year. They can start the application process earlier if there is any reason to hurry.

Each year, it seems, the U.S. Government makes some changes to the application process. Over the years, we have found that the process has actually gotten simpler. All application forms are now in PDF format on the USCIS website (www.uscis.gov). You can fill out and save these newest forms. This offers the convenience to copy information between members of the family and reduce your workload.

Briefly, here is the overall process with approximate pricing:

1. Obtain a passport photo for each member of the family. Walgreens offers this service conveniently and the price is reasonable, $8.99 for a set of two photos.

2. Gather the immunization records for each member of the family. You must present these records for a signature from the civil surgeon. Check with your agency for the appropriate medical office and costs. If any members of the family still need immunizations, please get them immunized and documented before visiting the civil surgeon. This will simplify the process.

3. Photocopy the I-94 cards, social security cards, and employment verification cards.

4. Photocopy their signed lease and other documents that prove they have been residents for at least one year.

5. Make sure all the necessary application forms are completed and signed. You may need to interview the family to get appropriate answers since some of the questions involve

parents' name, birthplaces, and dates of birth and death. (Form I-485 and possibly G-325 will be necessary. Fees are waived for refugees.)

6. Gather all employment information and government assistance information.

7. Have a check for fingerprinting made out to USCIS. Normally the charge is $70 for every person over 14, but this is waived for refugees.

8. Mail the entire packet of all of the above to the appropriate USCIS processing office and wait.

9. Two to four months later, they will need to have follow-up fingerprinting.

10. Up to two years later, a "Green Card," the Lawful Permanent Resident card, will arrive.

Overall, this is a rather time consuming project of information gathering, form filling and transporting.

Citizenship

Eventually the day comes. One of your refugee family members decides to take the next step and become a legal citizen of the United States. They relinquish the citizenship of the country they were born in, and they become Americans just like you and me.

If you have the chance to witness the oath, do it! Most likely, you were born here, a citizen by default, not by choice. It is a wonderful experience to see a group of immigrants committing their lives and joining this grand nation as equals. It stirs a spirit of patriotism to know that others truly have a longing to lead the type of life that we take for granted.

As of this writing, it has been nearly ten years since our first refugee family arrived. Several years ago, the father in our first resettlement case took this final step to become a citizen. At the federal courthouse in Milwaukee, he joined 71 other immigrants, from about 20 countries, to partake in a naturalization ceremony lasting about 30 minutes. As he held his right hand in the air, and the judge read the words of the oath, tears welled up in my eyes. I was recalling the joys and the pains that led up to this moment, the friendship with him and his family, and how well they've done in adapting to life here. I was proud of their accomplishments and ours too, as a resettlement team. That was a red-letter day.

CHAPTER 11

MAINTAINING & CELEBRATING SUCCESS

I became the man of our family when my father was killed. We became refugees. After living in a camp for several years we came to the United States. I tried to help my mom and sisters as much as I could, but I was only a teenager. One day after living here for a couple years we got a phone call from back home. Someone claimed that my father was found alive! After further struggle that was confirmed. We were able to have telephone conversations from time to time. Eventually my father was able to join us in our new home. Imagine thinking your dad was dead for seven years and then being reunited.

Of utmost importance throughout the resettlement process, is taking care of yourself and the other members of your committee. It is hard to give proper care to a refugee family in a meaningful and rewarding way, if your own life and health suffer as a result. It is wonderful to help a new family, but you must continue to care for yourself first.

You are about to engage in a unique process that can be very exciting. You may be swept into the thrill and emotion of doing something really good. You may become drawn into helping the refugee family at every possible moment and inserting yourself into their lives. The desire to do this is normal and can be positive, but you must limit yourself. Too much of a good thing may not be very good.

In the beginning, your refugee family will want your assistance often. Since you respond with love and compassion, they may ask for more. They might even start to test the limits. You want to be friends and you want them to like you. You may soon feel obligated to do more than what you originally signed on for. If this starts to happen, you must set some reasonable, and consistent, boundaries. Do not neglect other responsibilities in your own life.

Besides infringing on your life, giving too much assistance to your refugee family can also begin to create the wrong impression of your role from their perspective. They might come to think you receive payment to help them or that the U.S. government provided you to fulfill their every need. They are trying to make sense of their new life and you might not be able to explain adequately what a volunteer is and what you are supposed to do.

In order for your refugee family to become self-sufficient, they must be encouraged and empowered to live their own lives. Yes, help them do things that they have never encountered before. Help them work through "the system." Ultimately, let them make their own decisions. Let them succeed on their own. Let them stumble too so that they can learn how to move on. Your continuous unending care will not speed them to independence. They will only become dependent upon you. How much harder will it be on you, and them, to let go then?

When thinking about the boundaries you need to set, reflect upon the declining support model presented in chapter 3. You need to understand that you are helping a lot at first, but less and less as time goes on. If you feel called upon more and more, then something is wrong. Assess the situation and make adjustments. Remind yourself of this often as it is in your best interest and in the best interest of your refugee family.

Here are some boundaries that may make sense for you and your resettlement team. Please discuss and decide the appropriate boundaries for your group. You can establish others, ideally in advance of the refugees' arrivals, but don't be afraid to adjust as needed during the process.

- Decide that no individual members of your committee will go beyond their commitments without first discussing with their team, the chairperson, or the entire committee. If the family is asking you to do something you know is outside the normal role, you can politely tell them that you have to discuss with the team first. You are part of a team and you must respect the decisions of the team, including any established boundaries.

- While it is convenient for the family to have your pictures and phone numbers early on, they could take advantage of this later, using it as a calling list to get help. Establish the parameters around who should be called and why. Help them understand that they cannot call for every little concern, want, or need. Also, be sure they understand that 911, not you, is the right call for true emergencies.

- Refer the family members to medical professionals when needed. Remember they can get access to interpreters over the telephone so they can communicate well. You should not dispense medicine unless their physician has instructed you to help or monitor their situation.

- Refer the family members to appropriate psychological care and social services agencies when needed. They may have problems that professionals must handle. You will burn yourself out trying to "fix" a mental condition.

- Do not accept money from the family unless they are simply reimbursing an expense that you have already paid for on their behalf. Alternatively, decide that you won't ever buy something on their behalf and therefore they will never owe you money. Related to this, you might want to establish that you never loan the family any money.

- Learn to say "no." As they become more independent, they will have others they can call on. And, as they have to solve problems on their own, they will learn more about how to get things done.

- Stop providing basic transportation within three months. If you are still driving the family to work, school, and every appointment after the first few months then it is time to get them into carpools, on the bus, or other public transportation. Or help them get a driver's license and a car. It's time to let go.

If you give too much, going beyond your boundaries, ignoring your own family or responsibilities, you will eventually become very unhappy, potentially exhausted, or burned out. If you reach this condition, you are likely to quit and have negative feelings toward refugee resettlement or even the refugee family. Certainly, you would never volunteer for another resettlement project.

To help avoid burnout you need to maintain good communication with other members of your team. Discuss areas that you feel may have been outside the boundaries. Review your roles and expectations. Feel OK about griping a bit, with the idea to come up with solutions creatively. Don't complain simply to complain, as this solves nothing and can bring down others. Work for solutions that get you and your team back on track.

If the feelings of frustration or conflict exist within your team, you need to have some open and honest dialog between team members. Again, work toward resolution. Bashing other team members in front of others or behind their backs solves nothing and may build walls against someone. That does not support your needs. The loss of one person can negatively affect your group performance, making it harder for everyone else.

Finally, focus on success! You have done a lot. Your refugee family has grown increasingly independent. You feel like you can breathe again, engaging in your own life. Your refugee resettlement team has accomplished much in a relatively short amount of time. Celebrate it!

Some ideas of things you can do to celebrate:

- Send thank you cards to everyone who contributed. It can be fun to include a photo of the refugee family, with all of their names, and have copies of their signatures or even a short message in their own language and alphabet. Have it written in English too.

- Have a special meal or snack time where the refugee family prepares an ethnic dish for everyone to try. This would be a celebration along with the family.
- Anytime you have a full committee meeting, go around the group and allow each person to share one interesting thing that happened or something they learned about the family.
- Just have a party. Invite all members of the resettlement committee. Just celebrate with no expectations. People will talk about some of the fun things that happened, but that's not a requirement.
- Have a welcome reception. The refugee family prepares an ethnic dish or two for a group that is larger than your committee. Invite all those who contributed in any way. This might be something you do at church or with your larger group body whatever it is.
- Help the refugee family celebrate with you, their way. They will likely welcome any opportunity to say thank you to your resettlement team and anyone else who helped get them started. Ask for their ideas. In the past we've had families show their appreciation in these ways:
  - singing and dancing at church or at a party
  - preparing dinner in their home
  - inviting us to their traditional family celebrations and holidays
  - making presents and cards
  - sharing their personal stories to small groups or at church
  - giving ethnic gifts such as clothing or memorabilia from their homeland

CHAPTER 12

THINGS YOU WILL DISCOVER

We fled our homeland to a neighboring country. Even in this country we learned that government agents were hunting for us. We had to go into hiding, traveling secretly at night. Even though we had obtained official exit papers, allowing us to leave this country as refugees for the United States, we were warned that we might be intercepted on our way out. The authorities, if they caught up to us, were committed to sending us back to our home country even though that would present a great chance of losing our lives.

My wife expresses it best. "Refugee resettlement is wonderful, even in the most difficult moments. Each thing we learn helps us with the next family that we work with. Of course, every new family is unlike any previous. So just when you think you know what to expect, the next time it will be completely different."

Sponsoring refugees allows you to interact with people who are much different from yourself. Even if times had been good for these families, they grew up in a different environment. They developed different ways of thinking and reacting to the world around them. Your dealings with someone who thinks differently can be frustrating. However, it can be a strong catalyst to teaching you tolerance. In today's world of change and new peoples moving in next-door, tolerance is a good trait to have. Tolerance and understanding go hand in hand. If you can tolerate someone, along with their beliefs and practices, you can learn from them and begin to understand their perspective. Likewise, as you begin to understand them, their tolerance of you increases, and they begin to understand you. This can broaden into mutual respect and acceptance. As a result, a small bit of the world becomes a better place.

Religious freedom is a right we have in this country. Refugees might come from a different religious background. Working with them can help you become more aware of other beliefs and religions in the world. It can be fun gaining a greater understanding of the world around you.

A successful refugee resettlement program is not based on the family joining your church or group. The measure of success is based on your guidance getting them to be independent, making decisions, and living within a community. When they become self-sufficient, you know that your efforts were successful. Nothing else matters.

That said, refugee resettlement could be a rewarding ministry for a congregation. Churches often have a pool of talent available to meet the different roles needed in the resettlement process. Furthermore, refugee resettlement becomes an opportunity for a church to think outside its own walls without traveling to foreign lands.

Acts 1:8 says, *"But you will receive the power when the Holy Spirit comes on you; and you will be my witnesses in Jerusalem, and in all Judea and Samaria, and to the ends of the earth."*

Refugee resettlement gives us a chance to have an impact on the world, one family at a time. Maybe it doesn't seem like helping one family will make a difference in a problem that touches millions. Nevertheless, it does make a tremendous difference for that one family. You are offering a life-saving gift. Even if the family is not Christian, and you never have the opportunity to share your faith, you are still showing the love of Christ. You are a witness, a missionary, carrying out the vision that Jesus gave to His disciples. You will see the Holy Spirit at work.

Whether you live in a big city or a rural community, you might view your role as small, wondering what impact you can have on the world. Consider what can be accomplished if we reach out beyond ourselves beaming with the light of Christ. What difference can we make then, with that power? We are participating in the worldwide mission field without even leaving home.

Love does not recognize borders or distance. Prayer isn't stopped because it encounters an ocean. Grace isn't withheld because of a war somewhere.

We've been given the shoes of peace and it's our responsibility to put them on and lace them up. Jesus didn't tell us to find someone else to do it. It's our job to carry God's message beyond the walls of our church building, our neighborhood, our city, our state, and even our country. This is precisely what a refugee resettlement ministry is all about.

What difference can you make in the world? All the difference.

Repeat as needed.

CLOSING THOUGHTS

AN UNRESOLVED CASE

We are young and wanted to express our feelings, our views to what was not going well in our country. We knew things had to change. By expressing our feelings we got the attention of the government and now we are wanted. We tried to hide as many times as we could, but we failed. We decided to escape the country. We made it to a refugee camp and have registered with UNHCR. We are still afraid because people here have recognized us. We are anxious to be resettled and start new lives.

The moving and insightful story at the beginning of each chapter represents a family who has successfully arrived in the U.S. as refugees. As we have gotten to know the families, we learned their stories. But unlike their stories, the one presented here is a story in progress. Resettlement has not yet begun.

The person writing these words, and his friends, are living in a refugee camp. I have confirmed their registration through a UNHCR resettlement consultant in the camp. The camp is overloaded with refugees waiting to go through the eligibility process. In fact, the camp is so overloaded that right now, in early 2011, they are still processing cases of refugees who arrived in the 1990s. Unless something changes, there is no chance that these newly arrived refugees will be deemed as eligible to be presented to DHS/USCIS for many years to come.

While many refugees learn to be survivors, and I expect these young men will be, it is shameful that their prime years of life will be relegated to survival instead of productivity. Here are people excited to jump into a new environment and get on with their lives. But with the overloaded system, thousands of refugees ahead of them, and no way to move to a less crowded camp, they will likely live for years as a burden on, rather than a contribution to, society.

With more of us actively engaged in refugee resettlement, the success rates can rise, the outcomes improve, and attention can be given to more refugees in a timelier manner.

The story of these young men repeats itself over and over again. Without each of us taking some action, that number of 10 million refugees around the world won't change much. Right now, it holds nearly constant from year to year. With each of us taking action, however, that number isn't so big. With lots of attention, we might find ways to speed up every point of the process causing the number of refugees to dwindle rapidly. Imagine that every refugee who is eager to start over could start over, making a positive contribution in the receiving country.

I've seen it happen in small numbers. Together we can make a big impact!

A refugee family from Darfur and their makeshift shelter in eastern Chad. The United States will accept hundreds of the most vulnerable for resettlement.

Makeshift shelters and new tents at the new arrivals section of IFO camp, Dadaab, Kenya. Continuing violence in Somalia has led to more and more Somalis seeking refuge across the border in Kenya, but UNHCR is struggling to cope with the thousands of new arrivals at the camps who need shelter, food, and medical attention.

This young Karen family contemplate their new home in a refugee camp, Mae Ra Ma Luang.

Children play in front of a shelter provided by UNHCR in the north-eastern province of Takar. The agency provides home building material to the most vulnerable returnees. These children were born and raised in the Jalozai refugee camp in Pakistan.

Refugee children from Myanmar play in front of one of three nursery schools built and equipped with ninemillion.org funds in Tham Hin refugee camp on the Thai-Myanmar border.

Newly arrived refugee family has arrived at the airport near their resettlement community. The father/husband is carrying the tell-tale IOM bag.   Photo by J. Kirk

Recently resettled refugee family proudly standing in front of their first vehicle.

Photo by W. Houston

Young refugee, excited to show off his new car, stopped by for a visit.

Photo by J. Kirk

Crowded Milwaukee courtroom for a naturalization ceremony welcoming more than 70 new citizens including one of our former refugees.   Photo by J. Kirk

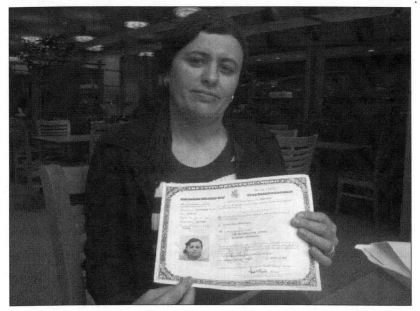

A former refugee, now American citizen, shows off her new certificate of naturalization.
Photo by I. Richards

APPENDIX A

FREQUENTLY ASKED QUESTIONS

1. "I've heard a lot about illegal immigrants/aliens. Aren't we trying to keep them out?"

Refugees are not illegal immigrants. They are indeed immigrants, as is any foreign-born individual who comes to the U.S. and stays here. But, refugees arrive in our country legally with full support from our government. They arrive with "refugee" status that allows them most rights that we enjoy as citizens. They can work, have access to social programs and benefits, and pay taxes like the rest of us. The only thing they cannot do initially is leave the U.S. with a guarantee of being allowed back in. In time, they can get authorization to leave and return. And, if they decide to naturalize someday, then they can even vote. They are generally excited to begin a new life in our country. One day their descendants will be as American as the rest of us.

2. "Will the refugees speak English?"

You should not expect them to. Some refugees may have learned English in their life before becoming refugees. Others may have had an opportunity to learn some English after they learned they would be coming to the United States. In any case, they are not likely to know much English, and their accent may be difficult to understand. With a little exposure they may be able to understand you more than what they can speak. However, don't count on this. Consider it a bonus if they have any English ability.

3. "Will the refugees be healthy?"

Before refugees leave their temporary home country, each has a health exam. If they have any kind of communicable disease, they will not be permitted to depart for the U.S. However, there are certain conditions that are admitted entry. For example, if one of your refugee family members was shot or injured in war they may have ongoing pain, physical limitations, or may even need periodic care to help them stay healthy. Other conditions might simply be missed.

Regardless of their condition when they arrive, it is expected that you will attend to their immediate needs. They enter the U.S. with health insurance coverage so don't worry about expense.

4. "I heard some refugees are allowed into the country with TB. Is that true?"

No. They would not knowingly be allowed to enter the United States with active tuberculosis. Furthermore, all refugees are required to have a health screening within 30 days of entry into the U.S. During that screening many refugees will show a positive skin test for TB. Even this does not mean that they have active TB that can spread. It is possible they were exposed to TB at some point in the past or, in many cases, it simply means they have had a past TB vaccination. To be on the safe side they will go through follow-up testing. If any concerns remain, they will be given medication so that neither you nor they will have to worry any longer.

5. "Can we select the refugee family that we want to co-sponsor?"

Depending on the rules of the agency you work with, and the current resettlement workload, you may have some say as to what country of origin you might prefer. For some resettlement groups, families of a particular size might be another option. But generally you will not have the opportunity to look at a family or their biography and then decide if you want to help. You should also not consider their religion as a determining factor in resettlement. It could be that their religion contributed to their being refugees in the first place. They need someone who can love them for who they are. Be open to the experience you are going to get and accept whatever family comes when you are ready. Enjoy the adventure.

6. "What will the family expect when they arrive?"

While still overseas, they will have an orientation session. They are told that sponsors will be waiting for them upon their arrival. They will have some understanding of what your resettlement committee's purpose is. But, regardless of what they've been told they will also have preconceived notions they have heard from others, or have pictured about the U.S. You should spend a little time with the adults in your refugee family, within the first day or two, with an interpreter, to give them your perspective and learn a little about theirs. This will also give them a chance to ask you questions that help clarify your role.

7. "The family that's coming is not Christian, but we are a church group. Can we pick a Christian family instead?"

No. We are aware of churches that refuse to take a family unless they receive a guarantee that the family is Christian. This is not right. Christ did not come to tell us to love only people like us. He came to love us all. As Christians, we are to love our neighbor as ourselves. These refugees are our neighbors. Show them the love of Jesus by demonstrating that love, regardless of their religion. At the same time you allow yourself to grow through learning and understanding. You become a better person, and by doing so, improve the world. Regardless of whether your refugee family carries your religious values or not, remember that your efforts are all about love.

8. "We are a church group. Can we expect the refugee family will become members of our church?"

No. While it is natural for you to want to share your faith if that is important to you, you must not force your beliefs upon your refugee family. If you and they already share the same faith then they might want to attend your church as a way of saying thanks. Do not require this however. Eventually they may meet others of their own ethnicity and join them where they worship. This is OK. If the family does not share your beliefs, you must not try to convert them. Often they have given up everything in life becoming refugees. Their religion may be one reason they were persecuted in their home country. Maintaining it may be the reason they fled. For them to be successful in the U.S. they must feel safe practicing their faith. Trying to convert a refugee to your faith is strictly prohibited by federal rules. If that is your intent, do not get involved with refugee resettlement.

9. "I am particularly concerned about the apartment lease; did you sign a one year lease by yourself or did your pastor sign on behalf of the church?"

For an apartment lease, we've done a variety of things depending on the circumstances at the time of the refugee family's arrival. The first two times we signed the lease on behalf of the refugee families because we made the arrangements prior to their arrival. For the next two families it worked out that they were already here when the paperwork needed to be signed so we didn't sign at all. More recently, we had the apartment on hold until the family arrived and could sign for themselves. But, even with the first two, the families eventually signed the lease on their own, with our church being listed as a cosigner. (Generally, I would not recommend cosigning unless it's your only option.)

Our pastors have never been involved in this process. In fact, I recommend that you carry out the entire refugee resettlement without assistance from church staff, unless of course they have volunteered to be a part of your team. We don't want the pastors to feel obligated to perform any tasks. They're busy enough already. For the first two leases, I signed on behalf of the church. Note that I have never discussed our signing or cosigning with the refugee families. We set the expectation that they are responsible for, and must pay, their own rent. We will help them for a time, but ultimately it is their responsibility. There are certain things, and this is one, that are not a choice for the refugee family. This minimizes risk to our church and us.

Also, be sure to check with your supporting agency, as they will want to minimize your risk as well, potentially making all of the arrangements through the agency.

10. "Did the teams handle everything by themselves or did you have to micro-manage all the teams yourselves?"

Regarding delegation, we expect every team to handle all details of their tasks without requiring micromanagement. As the chairperson of the refugee resettlement group, they should report to you so that you can coordinate activities with the various groups, perhaps keeping a master calendar of activities so that various teams don't schedule overlapping appointments, but you should not have to hold their hands through each step of the process. Managing all details would overwhelm the chairperson. For the chairperson to survive, he or she must trust each team to handle their tasks. If problems arise within a team they could ask the chairperson to help get others involved, but should not expect the chairperson to take over.

11. "What happens if nothing works right?"

There is one really good reason that you should not worry about this. But before I give the answer, let me first go over some things that you might be worried about:

a) What if I put together a team and I can't count on anyone?

b) What if I end up doing this all alone?

c) What if we still can't figure out this process?

d) What if the family is impossible to work with?

e) What if...? What if...? What if...?

Here's the big answer you need to keep in mind. The Volag, the resettlement agency that takes this case, is ultimately responsible. You are not. In other words, if you follow the guidance in this book, you get to take credit for the success, but not the failure, of any outcome. The work you and your team are doing is extremely beneficial to give the greatest possible chance of success for the refugee families you work with. I cannot emphasize that enough. But, if all else fails, discuss the situation with your contact at the agency. They can offer advice. They can help get you the resources you need. They can even take over or redirect the case to another team. Please do not be overcome by the "what ifs." In most cases the "wow, we really did it!" wins out.

12. "Do you take off work during the first week that the refugee family arrives?"

The first answer is no. We have never officially taken off work. I figure the refugees need to understand our workday and work ethic and that what we are doing for them is not dictated by our government but is given voluntarily. We do not expect anyone, on any of our teams, to commit so much time that it would require time away from work. We fit stuff around all of our schedules as much as possible. That said, it is good to have a few people in the resettlement group who are retired or are stay-at-home moms or dads or who can be flexible in their jobs to get away for an hour or two once in a while. Obviously various appointments that the refugees attend will be during business hours. Even when the families stayed in our home, we said good-bye in the morning and saw them when we returned later. The first couple days it was good to return at lunch to help them out and make sure they had something to eat, but otherwise we left them alone or had arranged for other people to take them to their appointments.

13. "Do you have children who cheerfully cooperate with this whole process?"

Bryn and I have two children. They are now 13 and 16 years old. They were not quite four and seven when we had our first refugee family move in with us for a week. Young children are awesome in that they don't have the social barriers that adults seem to feel. Lack of common language doesn't seem to matter to them. We've also found that all the refugee families understand what it's like to raise children so their presence produced a common bond. I can say that our children do cooperate with the process, though not always cheerfully. Now that they've gotten older, they did not want another family staying at our house. And, even though the children in more recent refugee families were about the same ages as our own, our kids did not play without inhibitions anymore. What I don't know is if we've just worn them out by dragging them along to every refugee related meeting and event for 10 years or if it's just that with age, they are becoming more conscious of differences and difficulties. It's my hope that at least they understand that it is important to help people of the world. To many refugees we are the embodiment of America and perhaps the only face of Jesus they've ever known. If our children learn this about our involvement then it's worth it.

14. "How do we let go after 6 months?"

Letting go is an important part of the process. From the beginning you must set the expectation that your assistance is temporary. You are here to help your refugee family learn the things they need in order to survive. It is not your responsibility to create a new dependent for yourself. Your ability to help another refugee family, or simply to return to life as it was, depends on your ability to finish the task you started. If the 6-month time comes and goes and you do not see a way out, it is time to start providing some "tough love." When you get the phone call that help is needed you'll have to suggest they find a different way to solve it. When they need a ride, you'll have to suggest a bus, taxi, or another friend of theirs. Refugees have taken care of themselves for years. Honestly, they can handle life in United States without your constant attention. Love them and let them go.

APPENDIX B

TEAM SKILLS AND TASKS CHECKLIST

Chairperson or Co-Chairpersons

Objective: Guide the entire refugee resettlement process to a successful outcome.

Skills required:
1. Task delegation
2. Organizational skills
3. Cross-cultural sensitivity
4. Patience and flexibility
5. Joyfulness

Task list:
___ Sign a co-sponsorship commitment or similar agreement form.
___ Be the main point of contact between your resettlement team and the sponsoring agency.
___ Put together your refugee resettlement team with a group committed to the appropriate resettlement activities.
___ Divide your committee members into appropriate teams.

___ Schedule and lead regular meetings. At first, since there will be much to report, you may want weekly meetings. As the refugees start to settle in, less frequent gatherings will be sufficient.

___ Establish various ways to communicate with your resettlement team.

___ Work with all the teams as the resettlement project progresses to ensure that all tasks are performed in a timely manner.

___ Find someone to step up if the assigned person(s) are unable to complete their tasks.

___ Meet the refugees at the airport (or find someone who can).

___ Put together a phone list of everyone on the resettlement committee and provide to the refugee family upon arrival.

___ Perform some level of orientation for the family upon arrival.

___ Ensure that housing requirements are met, and be available for the inspection.

___ Track the time, mileage, and expenses of all of your resettlement team volunteers.

___ Seek ways to plug the refugees into existing communities.

___ Celebrate the successes!

Housing Team

Objective: Secure suitable housing for your refugee family.

Skills required:
1. Willingness to make a lot of phone calls
2. Friendly open manner to talk to potential landlords
3. Sense of urgency
4. Decisiveness

Task list:
Preferably prior to arrival:

___ Look for affordable housing.

___ Look for safe housing.

___ Look for suitable housing.

___ Arrange for occupancy of the housing.

___ Prepare their home for arrival.

After arrival:

___ Provide the family with a way to make emergency phone calls.

___ Provide the family with some "walking around money."

___ Have utilities turned on in the name of the family.

___ Provide new home orientation.

___ Show family how to do laundry.

___ Order telephone service.

___ Provide a set of basic tools.

Furnishings Team

Objective: Furnish acquired housing with all required items.

Skills required:

1. Organization of needs list
2. Coordination with donors

Task list:

___ Put together a complete list of required furnishings and household items.

___ Add some nice optional furnishings.

___ Seek volunteers to provide needed items.

___ Make arrangements to get furnishings to the refugees' new home.

___ Keep track of all items as they are delivered.

___ Watch for extra needs and make arrangements to resolve them.

Required items:

___ One bed (frame, box spring, mattress) for each family member

___ At least one set of drawers for clothing, ideally one for each bedroom

___ One kitchen table with one chair for each family member

___ Enough living room seating for each member of the family

___ Appropriate lighting in each room

___ If family has an infant, provide appropriate items for sleeping, sitting, and eating

___ A stove, oven, and refrigerator

___ At least one sauce pan, one frying pan, and one baking dish

___ A set of mixing/serving bowls

___ A set of cooking and serving utensils

___ At least one place setting for each member of the family

- fork
- spoon
- knife
- plate
- bowl
- cup

___ A can opener

___ A fire extinguisher (not required if there are overhead sprinklers)

___ One bath towel for each member of the family

___ One set of sheets and blankets for each bed

___ Extra blankets if you live in a cold environment

___ One pillow and one pillowcase for each person

___ Dish soap

___ Bathroom/kitchen cleanser

___ Cleaning cloths and/or sponges

___ Laundry detergent

___ At least 2 wastebaskets

___ A broom and/or mop

___ Trash bags

___ Toilet paper

___ Shampoo

___ Soap (deodorant soap may be a good idea)

___ One toothbrush for each member of the family

___ Other personal hygiene items as appropriate for age and sex of family members

___ An alarm clock

___ Paper, pens/pencils, scissors.

___ Some spending money

Food Team

Objective: Stock the kitchen for the first 30 days.

Skills required:
1. Patience
2. Tolerance
3. Willingness to communicate without certainty of being understood
4. Price sensitivity
5. Ability to teach

Task list:
___ Organize donation of dry and canned goods.

___ Provide a hot meal for the family upon arrival.

___ Take family shopping the day after their arrival.

___ Grocery shopping trips throughout first 30 days.

___ Ongoing assistance even when family has their own money.

___ Explain frozen and packaged items.

___ Teach how to live on a budget.

___ Introduce to American foods.

Clothing Team

Objective: Provide adequate clothing for each family member for all occasions.

Skills required:
1. Patience
2. Willingness to shop with little common language
3. Ability to say "no" when asked for unnecessary goods

Task list:
___ Provide adequate clothing for all occasions.

___ Provide diapers for children under the age of 2.

___ Make sure clothing is culturally appropriate.

___ Teach family to use washing machine and dryer.

Medical Care Team

Objective: Assure that all family members receive needed medical attention.

Skills required:
1. Willingness to make decisions on behalf of someone who is putting their trust in you
2. Tolerance for being unable to explain everything you feel is necessary

Task list:
___ Sign HIPAA confidentiality forms.

___ If present in your community, contact the public health department to see if there are any necessary health screenings.

___ If there is no public health screening, make sure a private physician gives a thorough exam.

___ Follow up with recommended immunizations, medicines, or other actions.

___ Work through medical emergencies if/when they come up.

___ Schedule dental appointments as soon as possible.

___ If there are mental health issues, refer the case to your supporting agency.

___ Help family select employer health insurance options.

Employment Team

Objective: Prepare all employable adults for work, and help with job hunting.

Skills required:
1. Patience
2. Willingness to have tough, honest, and open discussions with your refugee family
3. Ability to deal with employers who may not be tolerant
4. Patience (yes, you need more patience)

Task list:
___ Set the mental groundwork for employment, setting them up for success.
___ Show the family the cost of everything they will have to pay on a monthly basis, e.g. rent, utilities (gas, electric, water), food, airfare, telephone, medical bills, misc.
___ Show benefits (food stamps, other assistance) and how this falls short of needs.
___ Show how much money they will make at a job (start low, $7.25/ hour minimum).
___ Demonstrate that this wage will cover their bills.
___ Show that your group will help them cover costs while job hunting.
___ Interview the refugees to evaluate their skills and interests.
___ Write up simple resumes if needed.
___ Fill out job applications when needed.
___ Orient them to the American workplace.
___ Take the family members to interviews.
___ Help figure out transportation to the job.
___ Check into childcare assistance, if needed.

Education Team

Objective: Enroll all children in school and all adults in English classes.

Skills required:
1. Tolerance of language gaps
2. Willingness to mediate between educational institutions and the family

Task list:

___ Enroll adults in English language classes or find tutors to teach English as a second language.

___ If necessary, provide childcare while parents are attending their English classes.

___ Enroll children in appropriate level schooling; whether daycare, preschool, or public school.

___ Provide basic school supplies, as required, for all children enrolled in school.

___ Assist the children with homework assignments, or help them get appropriate tutoring or other assistance when needed.

___ Assist the children and parents in understanding any notes or other information that might be sent home from school.

___ Be an advocate for the family with teachers and school officials. It makes their job easier if they know they can contact you with any issues.

___ Encourage the family to be involved in the community and attend any school activities and meetings that would involve their children.

___ Provide feedback to the rest of your resettlement committee regarding any cultural issues you may learn about the refugee family.

Transportation Team

Objective: Provide transportation for your refugee family until they can make their own arrangements.

Skills required:
1. Calendar management
2. Comfortable speaking to someone who may not understand your language
3. Comfortable traveling in silence

Task list:
____ Welcome the family at the airport, unless the chairperson is already handling this.
____ Provide, or arrange for, transportation to various functions.
____ Teach applicable transportation laws such as use of seat belts, infant/toddler seats, no children in front seats, etc.
____ Provide with infant/toddler seats for each applicable child.
____ Teach how to use public transportation, if available.
____ Show the children how to use school buses if this is how they will get to school.
____ If bicycles would be useful and desired, solicit donations for used bikes or offer assistance in purchasing bikes.
____ Teach bicycle safety rules, and make sure helmets are used.
____ Help those of appropriate age obtain a driver's license.
____ Help with the purchase of a car when the time comes.
____ Explain insurance needs before the purchase.

Finance Team

Objective: Help family with money handling and financial decisions.

Skills required:
1. Understanding of finances
2. Ability to teach and/or demonstrate money matters
3. Desire to maintain records for your refugee committee

Task list:
___ Make sure that your group has sufficient funds for an initial housing security deposit, rent, food.
___ Ensure that refugees have some money to spend upon their arrival.
___ Determine their understanding of U.S. Currency, teaching coins and bills, if necessary.
___ Help your refugee family understand the expenses they are likely to see.
___ Demonstrate the importance of getting a job from a financial perspective.
___ Help them make realistic goals in regard to income.
___ Help the family open a checking account.
___ Teach how to write checks and balance a checkbook.
___ Help the family identify and understand bills that come in the mail.
___ Help them understand the importance of paying their bills on time.
___ Make sure they are able to file income taxes.
___ Keep detailed and accurate records of contributions and expenditures.
___ Provide reports to the resettlement agency that you are working with.
___ Reimburse members of your resettlement committee for out-of-pocket expenses.

Public Relations Team

Objective: Educate others on the importance of refugee resettlement.

Skills required:
1. Making signs or fliers
2. Talking to groups of people
3. Writing articles

Task list:

___ Prepare fliers and/or posters with information to generate interest in your project.

___ Speak in church or civic groups, put up posters, and solicit donations.

___ Keep people informed of your refugee family's progress.

___ Send thank-you notes to those who have donated.

___ Plan an event to introduce your refugee family to those who helped make their new life possible.

___ Handle the media if appropriate.

ABOUT THE AUTHOR

In 1991, Jeffrey Kirk stood in the central square of Kokshetau, Kazakhstan. At the front of a pressing crowd, he shook the hand of Mikhail Gorbachev, still leader of the USSR for a few more months. Who could have known how much the world would change in the next 20 years?

The Soviet Union collapsed and independent countries arose. Throughout most of the 1990s, Jeffrey followed up with return visits to Russia and Kazakhstan as part of a Sister City relationship. He saw the people going through hardships, yet he saw how most remained hopeful.

During these years, Jeff learned a lot about interacting with people of much different cultures. He learned about their unique struggles as their countries changed quickly, their common struggles as humans, and the hopes that all have for a better future. Through this experience, Jeff discovered the compassion, understanding, and sensitivity needed to work with individuals and groups coming from very different life experiences.

As his own family grew, it became more difficult to take international trips. Instead of heading off to the other side of the world, Jeff stayed closer to home. He joined cleanup efforts in Puerto Rico following Hurricane Georges. Again, he saw the hardship of the people, as well as the hope and gratitude in their eyes. Years later while contributing in both Mississippi and New Orleans after Hurricane Katrina, he had a similar experience... the witness of hardship and hope—and how people of compassion help alleviate the hardship and validate the hope.

Being a refugee is yet another story of hardship and hope; hardship of present circumstance and hope for a better future. Jeff views refugee resettlement as a means to play a role in the manifestation of hope. And, he could play the role without traveling anywhere. In other words, refugee resettlement offered an international experience without leaving home. He could work on the "hope" side of the equation by bringing people of the world to his door.

Jeff has resettled refugees since 2001, working with his wife, Bryn, through their church and Lutheran Social Services as the sponsoring agency. Their first refugee family arrived September 7, 2001. Four days later the five refugees and the four Kirks all sat glued to the TV watching in horror as the troubles of the world came to the United States.

Jeff's team has directly resettled eight families. He and his wife have also helped to assist and educate volunteers at other churches.

Jeff and Bryn have brought their children, Alexander and Victoria, into the refugee resettlement process as well. It has been a great teaching ground to demonstrate through personal action that it's good to help others. And, certainly just as important, children need to understand that the problems and concerns of "home" are but a small piece of today's global, interconnected reality.

Jeff and his family live in Waukesha, Wisconsin. They enjoy getting away from home to discover new places in the U.S. and other countries around the world. Family vacation time is something they all look forward to.

When not helping refugees or traveling, in his personal time Jeff enjoys bicycling, internet marketing, and helping business owners achieve success online.

RESOURCES

Recommended Reading:

- *Notes from My Travels*, Angelina Jolie
  Stories of visits with refugees in Africa, Cambodia, Pakistan, and Ecuador
- *The Middle of Everywhere*, Mary Pipher
  Stories of refugees who have made it out of camps and resettled in the U.S.

Other Resources:

Be sure to visit **www.resettlementsupport.com** for ongoing refugee resettlement discussion.

In addition, as a reader of this book, you can take advantage of free supplemental information including the:
- 8-month Resettlement Case Study
- Quick Bus Lesson
- Situational Judgment Exercise
- Communication without Language Exercise

These bonuses and more are available to you at:
www.10millionto1.com/extras

Made in the USA
Columbia, SC
12 July 2017